ENTREPRENEURSHIP MADE EASY

ENTREPRENEURSHIP MADE EASY

A MANUAL ON HOW THE WINNERS WIN AND WHY THE LOSERS LOSE

V.S.M. NAIR, G. VIJAYA RAGHAVAN, HARI S. NAIR

Notion Press

Old No. 38, New No. 6
McNichols Road, Chetpet
Chennai - 600 031

First Published by Notion Press 2016
Copyright © V.S.M. Nair, G. Vijaya Raghavan,
Hari S. Nair 2016
All Rights Reserved.

ISBN 978-1-946048-35-6

This book has been published with all efforts taken to make the material error-free after the consent of the author. However, the author and the publisher do not assume and hereby disclaim any liability to any party for any loss, damage, or disruption caused by errors or omissions, whether such errors or omissions result from negligence, accident, or any other cause.

No part of this book may be used, reproduced in any manner whatsoever without written permission from the authors, except in the case of brief quotations embodied in critical articles and reviews.

DEDICATION

To the millions of entrepreneurs who dare to dream
the impossible dreams to reach the unreachable stars

CONTENTS

About the Authors — ix
Authors' Note — xi
Foreword — xv
Preface — xvii

Part I
Exploring the Mystique of Entrepreneurship: An Analytical Framework

1. Entrepreneurship: An Intellectual Holy Grail — 3
2. Entrepreneurial Small Businesses: One Of Society's Greatest Resources — 7
3. The Entrepreneur: An Enigma Wrapped In A Mystery — 21
4. Unraveling The Mystique Of Entrepreneurship — 53
5. Why Do So Many Startups Die So Young? — 71
6. Entrepreneurial Success: Beating the Odds — 95

Part II
Winning the Battle for Survival

7. How Winners Win Customer Loyalty — 111
8. How Best to Manage Partners & Employees — 129
9. How Best to Manage Money — 133
10. How Best to Manage Operations — 147
11. Rules of Success Recommended by Those Who Succeeded — 153
12. 1 To 1 Billion: Seven Exponential Entrepreneurial Stories — 157
13. Entrepreneurship: The Widely Debated But Barely Understood Concept — 159

Part III

Impact of Social & Economic Environment on Entrepreneurship Development

14.	Impact of the Environment on Entrepreneurship Development	165
15.	Promoting Small Businesses: Policy Aids	177

Part IV

Business Opportunity Identification and Screening

16.	Business Opportunity Identification	195
17.	Idea Screening	201
18.	Ten Steps To Launching A Business	203

Part V

Business Plan: Purpose, Structure and Content

19.	Business Plans	207

Part VI

Is Entrepreneurship for You? Do You Have What It Takes?

20.	Testing for Entrepreneurial Prowess	221

ABOUT THE AUTHORS

Mr. V.S.M. Nair is a Post-graduate in Economics with over 50 years experience in consulting and venture promotion across institutions like National Council of Applied Economic Research, Tata Economic Consultancy Services and Kerala State Industrial Development Corporation. Since 1997, he has been the Managing Director of VMA Consultants Pvt. Ltd., a venture management and consulting company.

V.S. Madhavan Nair (vsmnair@gmail.com)

Mr. Vijaya Raghavan is a Graduate Engineer with over 35 years of professional experience. As the founding-CEO, he provided the leadership in conceptualizing, planning and creating Technopark Trivandrum, India's first Software Technology Park and one of the finest in Asia. He has also been the prime force behind the National Institute of Speech and Hearing (NISH), an initiative of the Kerala Government focusing on identification, rehabilitation, and education of individuals with communication disorders, which was accorded the status of a National University by the Government of India. Since 1997, he has been the President of VMA Consultants Pvt. Ltd.

G. Vijaya Raghavan

Mr. Hari S. Nair is a Graduate Engineer with a Masters in Business from the Indian Institute of Management, Calcutta. He has a few years of experience in management consulting with KPMG and in fund-raising & social media marketing with the Isha Foundation. Till recently, he was an Assistant Professor in charge of Marketing & Admissions at the Asian School of Business, Trivandrum. Currently, he is a consultant for VMA Consultants Pvt. Ltd. and is the Centre Head of Career Launcher, Trivandrum.

Hari S. Nair (hari.cet@gmail.com)

AUTHORS' NOTE

a. The term 'products' - appearing throughout this book - also means 'services'.

b. Men account for an overwhelmingly large proportion of entrepreneurs globally. However, we believe entrepreneurship should be gender-neutral. The terms he, his and him, therefore, could also mean she, hers and her.

c. **This Manual is essentially a calibrated compilation of widely known concepts and processes without any pretension whatsoever of it being an original, research-driven treatise.**

d. Although part of the narrative is set against the Indian context, most of the contents of the book have universal application.

e. This analytical framework has been designed as a Textbook. A wide range of headings and subheadings has, therefore, been provided for easy understanding.

DEFINITION OF MICRO, SMALL AND MEDIUM ENTERPRISES

MSMEs as defined by Government of India

Manufacturing sector

In the Manufacturing sector, the level of investment in plant and machinery is used by the Govt. of India to define whether an enterprise is a Micro, Small or Medium Enterprise.

Micro enterprises are those where the investment doesn't exceed Rs. 2.5 million. Small enterprises are those whose investment ranges from Rs. 2.5 million to Rs. 50 million. Medium enterprises are those in which the investment is between Rs. 50 million and Rs. 100 million.

Services sector

In the Services sector, the level of investment in equipment is used to define whether an enterprise is a Micro, Small or Medium Enterprise.

Micro enterprises are those where the investment doesn't exceed Rs. 1 million. Small enterprises are those whose investment ranges from Rs. 1 million to Rs. 20 million. Medium enterprises are those in which the investment is between Rs. 20 million and Rs. 50 million.

Government of India is in the process of enhancing the existing limits.

European Union Definition of MSMEs

EU uses three metrics to differentiate Micro, Small and Medium Enterprises - number of employees, turnover and balance sheet total.

Micro enterprises are those whose employees number less than 10 or with a turnover of less than € 2 million or a balance sheet total of less than € 2 million. Small enterprises are defined by number of employees ranging between 10 and 50, turnover or balance sheet total between € 2 million and € 10 million. Medium enterprises are those with between 50 and 250 employees, turnover between € 10 million and € 50 million or balance sheet total ranging between € 10 million and € 43 million.

In the USA, Small and Medium Enterprises are defined as those having less than 500 employees.

FOREWORD

Indians have had a long history of entrepreneurship, over millennia. Our organized societies and our ambitious and creative minds have resulted in a long legacy of enterprise, trade and commerce both within the sub-continent, as well as with far-off lands. Post-liberalization, the freeing up of controls and reduction in barriers to business have freed up more entrepreneurial energy in the country. The many new opportunities thrown up by leaps in technology, and the 'online world', too, have given fresh momentum to the wave of entrepreneurship in our country.

It is in this context, that I find **Entrepreneurship Made Easy: A Manual on How the Winners Win and Why the Losers Lose** a particularly timely and relevant work, by its respected authors. I am grateful for their kind request to me to write the Foreword and delighted to introduce this book to you.

Existing or aspiring entrepreneurs are a fascinating lot.

They need to have a healthy risk appetite, be innovative and productive, be nimble in their business practices, possess self-belief, and have 'staying-power' if they are called upon to do so during rough periods in their business life. With so much demanded of an entrepreneur, it is important to consider and recognize the answers to many questions, such as:

u) Is an entrepreneur 'born', or is he 'made'?

v) Is entrepreneurship an art, a science or a practice? Can it be taught, and therefore, learnt?

w) Does every entrepreneur need a 'breakthrough' product or service in order to succeed?

x) Is formal education a necessity for an entrepreneur?

y) Does size matter?

In Parts I & II, the authors examine these, and many more such questions that may exist in the minds of those fascinated by this topic. They point to the role of luck in the life of an entrepreneur, and to the near assuredness of failures along the way; failures that provide invaluable lessons for the entrepreneur's journey ahead.

They use a judicious mix of data, published reports and subjective evaluation to help the reader learn lessons, and draw conclusions. Their broader examination of the subject of entrepreneurship is tempered with a prescriptive, 'handbook' approach that would help entrepreneurs examine their present and their future, in practical terms. Through this method, the authors have attempted to address the many myths that surround the practice of entrepreneurship, and bring in a strong element of 'real life' lessons and experiences for the reader.

Part III of the book deals with the broader topic of the impact of the economic and social environment on entrepreneurship. It examines the overall business eco-system from policy frameworks to capital, technology and market access, access to talent and skills, and more. This section provides a useful canvas for any new entrepreneur to better examine the business context of his venture.

In Parts IV and V, the authors provide valuable tips, checklists and business plan templates that many new entrants into this community of entrepreneurs would find useful as a reference. One would agree that at the end of the day, it is only successful practice and implementation of ideas that really counts.

And this is where the value of this handbook would be felt the most. As a useful aid, in converting our entrepreneurial dreams into business realities!

Any aspiring entrepreneur will find merit in reading this book.

Dr. S. Ramadorai
Former Chairman, National Skill Development Corporation
Former Vice-Chairman and CEO, Tata Consultancy Services

PREFACE

Demographic dividend or demographic time bomb: The utterly contrasting scenarios confronting India

Although the estimates of employment or unemployment in the country vary from one source to another, the underlying trends are clear, compelling and, indeed, scary.

India has the largest "young population" in the world with 31% of the population in the age group of 0–14 years, close to 55% below 25 years and 64% in the working age group (15–64 years). By 2025, India will have the world's largest workforce (total number of people who **could be** employed); the number of youths in the age group of 15–29 alone in the workforce is estimated at 158 million.

The surging economically active working age population can theoretically contribute significantly to the economy by earning, spending and saving. With relatively limited spending on dependents, this phenomenon can yield impressive demographic dividends. This seemingly clear-cut relationship pre-supposes that the economy generates adequate number of sustainable, gainful jobs for those who enter the labour market. The emerging situation does seem to suggest that India may fail to fulfill this pre-condition.

Some of the disturbing aspects of India's employment scene include:

a) During the last 30 years, the rate of growth of employment was a fraction of the rate of growth of GDP. For instance, during the period 2004–05 and 2011–12, employment growth was 0.5% per annum as against GDP growth of 8.5% per annum; **almost jobless growth**.

b) Employment generation in agriculture and manufacturing (especially in the organized sector) has been stagnating for different sets of reasons. Data on Investment Intentions filed with Govt. of India by entrepreneurs promoting medium and large scale projects for 2014–15 indicate that the jobs proposed to be created will be less than one job per Rs. 10 million capital investments.

c) Nowhere is the demand for employment more severe and the obstacles more intractable than in rural areas that are home to about 70% of the country's population.

d) The growing employment opportunities in the services sector are not much of a help for the youths originating from the rural or semi-urban centers because of the mismatch between the skill sets required by the sector and what such youths possess.

e) The National Census of 2011 had estimated the number of youths in the age group of 15 to 24 who were unemployed or under-employed at a staggering figure of 47 million.

f) More than 90% of India's workforce belongs to the informal sector - most participants of the sector may not register themselves with any governmental agency or pay tax or minimum wages.

During the next 3-4 decades India will be adding more to its population than any other nation in the world. Estimates of the annual addition to the working age group vary significantly as between different sources. The general perception has been that the addition will be about 15 million per annum. A recent study by Kotak Institutional Securities, a leading Indian financial company, has estimated that about 240 million people will join the working age population during the next 10 years whereas the country may not add more than 100 million non-farm jobs during this period (unless fundamental reforms are unleashed across the economy). This study debunks the much-flaunted story of India's demographic dividends. What India could face is a demographic curse: A large number of unskilled and semi-skilled youngsters forming the bulk of the labour force with low productivity and lower wages.

If the rate of job creation follows the past pace, the unemployment situation can get truly unmanageable leading to unimaginable socio-economic distress.

a) It is argued that one of the factors that co-relates most strongly with instability is a bulge in the youth population. Societal upheaval is found to be proportional to the unemployment among young men and women aged 15-24.

b) According to a UN study ("*A Clash of Generations? Youth Bulges and Political Violence*" by Hendrik Undal for Population Division,

UN Department of Economic and Social Affairs, 2012), for every 1% point increase in the share of the population aged 15–24, the risk of civil war increases by 4%.

c) The Report of World Economic Forum, Global Risks, 2014 gives an ominous warning that the demographic "youth bulge" will raise the risk of social unrest by creating a disaffected "lost generation" (victims of youth unemployment) who are vulnerable to being sucked into criminal or extremist movement.

d) Joblessness is viewed as one of the triggers of the Arab Spring, starting with Tunisia's so-called Jasmine Revolution in early 2011, which tragically let loose unprecedented levels of deaths and destruction dragging the entire region into severe socio-political turmoil.

Entrepreneurship, India's destiny

The employment generation capacity of the agricultural and manufacturing sectors has to be enhanced by deploying the required resources, appropriate technologies and policy interventions including those fostering active private participation. **What is profoundly more critical is creating an ecosystem that will promote millions of Micro, Small and Medium Enterprises to generate millions of factory and non-factory jobs to absorb the millions of unskilled and under-skilled youths entering the labour pool.**

Almost 70% of India's working-age population has no education beyond primary school. Less than 3% of the workforce in India has undergone formal skill training as compared to 96% in South Korea, 80% in Japan, 68% in Britain and 75% in Germany. The best hope for the majority of working-age population to escape low-wage farm jobs is low- to mid-skilled jobs in small factories, shops, hotels and restaurants and, of course, self-employment, all overwhelmingly belonging to Micro, Small and Medium Enterprises **(MSMEs)** sector.

Extensive studies done by Small Enterprise Assistance Fund (www.seaf.com), a Washington-headquartered global fund management group, demonstrate that MSMEs represent a bulwark of political and economic stability. This is so because **MSMEs are a cost-effective delivery mechanism for poverty alleviation**.

The authors believe that creating and promoting an awareness of, and passion for entrepreneurship development, using every medium available, should be an article of faith of all informed individuals and institutions in India.

Focus of the book

This book is essentially about young, owner-managed, independent (non-subsidiary), entrepreneurial Startups promoted by a single promoter or a small founding team offering a new product to an existing or new market or an existing product to existing or new market.

Many Startups will eventually achieve the transition into bigger entities; most may lose the entrepreneurial spirit in the process. However, the focus of the book is on the phase when they are Startups belonging to MSMEs sector. It could be argued that business basics are scale-neutral; nonetheless, MSMEs have to deal with their own unique challenges and opportunities.

We are defining an entrepreneurial business in a very broad sense. Because, we believe that the promoter of even the least innovative venture has to continually make choices (relating to product features, process technology, pricing, distribution etc.) which have uncertain outcomes. In that sense, an entrepreneurial business could range from a mobile roadside eatery to a barbershop to a store to a school to a hospital to a manufacturing unit to a garage-born IT company with the potential to be a world-straddling titan like Apple Inc.

The book attempts to answer such questions as:

a) Who is an entrepreneur? Why is an entrepreneur, an entrepreneur?

b) Is he born or made?

c) What is entrepreneurship?

d) Is entrepreneurship learnable and, therefore, teachable?

e) Why do so many Startups die so young?

f) How do some win against impossible odds?

g) What lessons do we learn from the winners, and more importantly, from the losers?

h) What is the impact of the regulatory, economic and socio-cultural environment on the process of creating a robust entrepreneurial class?

i) How do we create the right ecosystem to foster small enterprises?

Isn't most everything you want to know about entrepreneur or entrepreneurship already known? Yes, almost. Enter the key words - entrepreneurship, entrepreneurial success, entrepreneurial failure etc. - and the Search Engine will release an avalanche of results, as stunning as the estimated 50 million or thereabout.

Well, that's the problem! How many of us have the time or the inclination to go trawling on such a vast and deep ocean of information? Not that the authors are claiming to have attempted such a terribly daunting, nearly impossible, task. However, they did make huge efforts to explore the vast expanse (overwhelmingly online sources) in an attempt at picking the right stuff, as was thought appropriate, to reflect on and learn from.

This analytical toolkit attempts to bring into play a wide range of insights, ideas or perspectives relating to entrepreneurship. The nuggets of insight on entrepreneur and entrepreneurship have been presented in such a format as to help unravel the 'known unknowns and unknown unknowns'.

How some entrepreneurs win or why many lose the battle for survival is at the heart of this book.

What is distinctive about the book?

One of the key differentiators of this book is that the content is organized into easily swallowable portions. The lean, lucid prose, devoid of most of the typical jargons, makes the presentation highly accessible to the readers.

Part of the presentation is in second person plural mode.

Who will benefit the most from the book?

The intended audience of this document includes faculty and students of business schools and engineering colleges, research scholars, those planning Startups, existing entrepreneurs, industry associations, bureaucrats concerned with promotion of enterprises, banks and other financial institutions mandated to stimulate the growth of MSMEs and venture capital groups.

Structuring of the book

The book has a 6-part structure. Part I is concerned with the core theme of entrepreneurship, including why most Startup fail. Part II discusses how the winners win. Part III is on the impact of social and economic environment on entrepreneurship development. Part IV is on business opportunity identification and screening. Part V is about Business Plans and Part VI attempts to answer the question whether one has what it takes to be an entrepreneur; a set of self-rating tests helps answer this question.

PART I

Exploring the Mystique of Entrepreneurship: An Analytical Framework

Entrepreneur: Individual

Entrepreneurial: Attitudes, skills and behaviours

Entrepreneurship/Entrepreneurialism/Entrepreneurism: Process

Enterprise: An organizational entity

1
Entrepreneurship: An Intellectual Holy Grail

Few areas of management science have attracted greater attention of economists, management teachers and practitioners, behavioural scientists and policy makers for the past over three decades or so than entrepreneur and entrepreneurship.

"Entrepreneurs have never been more in fashion. Politicians court them, the media glorify them and even our public admires their wealth and success. This adulation has a hard core of justification." - Robert Heller, in the foreword to the book *Entrepreneurship: The Seeds of Success* by John Forbat

Honored by Business Schools, nominated to top charities, celebrated in the popular press and studied by the new generation of potential entrepreneurs, successful entrepreneurs have acquired unparalleled importance in the recent years. The entrepreneurial community's success has attracted capital on a scale unthinkable in the past. But for a certain dip since 2008, Venture Capital and Initial Public Offerings have been growing exponentially, especially in the US. Successful entrepreneurs demonstrated their wisdom by investing their surpluses in Venture Funds and Angel Networks to nourish more entrepreneurial talents.

Field of entrepreneurship is ranked as one of the fastest growing areas in management literature over the last more than 15 years. Recent explosion of books (amazon.com lists about 6000 books relating to entrepreneurship) and magazines (nearly 50 English-language refereed academic journals on the subject are published in the USA), web sites and a wide range of University courses reflect the significant public interest in the subject.

In the US, academic programmes relating to entrepreneurship and the number of positions/Chairs in the Universities have increased dramatically. There are hundreds of Business Schools with majors in entrepreneurship. Many US Universities have developed PhD programmes in entrepreneurship. This trend has caught on in the rest of the world as well.

In India, the concepts of entrepreneurship and Startups have captured the nation's imagination and mindshare during the past three years or so more vigorously than ever before. Financial publications like The Economic Times have been celebrating the meteoric rise in the number of Startups, mostly in the IT space. The valuation of some of them has been scaling dizzying heights. Most of the business schools and engineering colleges and research centers are agog and are launching entrepreneurship clubs and Startup Incubators.

This nation-wide fervor inspired the Prime Minister of the country to make the clarion call, START UP INDIA, STANDUP INDIA, in his Independence Day oration on August 15th 2015.

Amidst such worldwide excitement, we need to come to terms with a somewhat uncomfortable truth: The subject of entrepreneurship is highly elusive, somewhat fuzzy and imprecise. It is, therefore, open to different shades of meanings and interpretations. After all, an entrepreneur is a very particular person and every enterprise is somewhat unique. Entrepreneurs do not necessarily fit a common mould. The very fact that many entrepreneurial traits are enveloped in behavioural terms does not make things any easier.

For instance, the prime motivation to pursue an incredibly challenging and utterly unpredictable career like entrepreneurship has always been explained in terms of the passion, joy and self-realization that creation and problem-solving give rise to. Guy Kawasaki in his book *The Art of the Start* defines the meaning of entrepreneurial development in terms of "Making the world a better place", "Increase the quality of life", "Right a terrible wrong" and "Prevent the end of something good".

Passion will take one only that far, if an enterprise is not commercially and financially viable. While having a dream and being passionate about it are important, an entrepreneur will end up in serious difficulty if he doesn't seek evidence of market potential of the offering. Making money need not necessarily be the prime motivation. Indeed, it has almost never been. But, one should not be carried away by one's passion and not be a calculating and rational businessperson. According to a 2012 article in the Harvard Business Review, an entrepreneur should seek *"the right balance between passion, patience and a practical respect for market feedback."*

The concept of entrepreneurship is clearly kaleidoscopic. That is, the entrepreneur sees the world through a kaleidoscope - constantly looking at it from different angles and seeing resources combined in different ways to address different needs. The world, in turn, looks at entrepreneurs and entrepreneurship from different perspectives, some of them at variance with each other, as the ensuing analysis amply demonstrates.

There has been a glut of hypotheses, theories, ideas and simplistic hunches trying to get to the core of this stubborn phenomenon. However, most such answers as have been proffered do not seem to be robust enough to be generalizable.

"Entrepreneurship is the modern-day philosopher's stone: a mysterious something that supposedly holds the secret to boosting growth and creating jobs." - Schumpeter Column, The Economist, July 2013

The study of entrepreneurship shall indeed remain an intellectual Holy Grail. This book marks the end of the authors' quest for this Holy Grail. For now!

Mind to Market: The Magic of Entrepreneurship

R&D creates technological knowledge or a new possibility through invention WHICH LEADS TO the new knowledge being transformed into innovation WHICH LEADS TO the innovation developing the new possibility to usefulness or marketability and breeding new business ideas WHICH LEADS TO the business ideas helping discover customers WHICH LEADS TO the commercialization of business ideas, a process driven by entrepreneurs, generating new (better or cheaper) products/services WHICH LEADS TO Creation of new jobs by the new businesses WHICH LEADS TO the injection of extra income into the economy WHICH LEADS TO the new income promoting more spending and new demand WHICH LEADS TO more production of products to meet the growing demand AND SO ON.

These powerful linear relationships represent a virtuous circle of economic well-being touching millions of lives!

2
Entrepreneurial Small Businesses: One Of Society's Greatest Resources

Entrepreneurs are a national treasure and should be protected, nourished and rewarded.

2.1 ENTREPRENEURSHIP: THE LIFEBLOOD OF ALL ECONOMIES

"A positive and robust correlation between entrepreneurship and economic performance has been found in terms of growth, firm survival, innovation, employment creation, technological change, productivity increases and exports." - European Economic and Social Committee.

Economists define the resources that go into production as land (natural resources), labour, capital and entrepreneur. The entrepreneur combines the first three of these to create products or provide service. In the absence of this function, the other resources - land, labour and capital - will remain idle.

Every country, whether developed or developing, needs entrepreneurs. Whereas a developing country needs entrepreneurs to initiate the process of development, the developed one needs entrepreneurs to sustain it.

Entrepreneurship is the engine fuelling innovation, employment generation and economic growth. It is the corner stone of the free enterprise system. In fact, even in China, unorganized and informal enterprises, operating outside State control are the most vibrant. Global Entrepreneurship Monitor has determined that variation in the rates of entrepreneurship may account for as much as one-third of the variations in economic growth across the world.

Unlocking the potential of growth-oriented micro, small and medium entrepreneurial businesses is the key to unleashing economic and social progress.

Technological knowledge, generated through public and private R&D, is increasingly the main source of economic growth. New knowledge, however, has little value to people unless it is applied to real world problems and challenges, a process driven by entrepreneurs.

New entrepreneurial firms are clearly a source of multiple benefits for the society as a whole. This explains why entrepreneurship has attracted worldwide acclaim. Some of these benefits are summarized below:

a) Entrepreneurship is a local and regional level activity and new firms, with short gestation period, can immediately begin to create benefits for their host locations unlike economic development interventions focusing on building massive projects that yield returns in the long run. MSMEs tend to use indigenous technologies and local resources. For capital-scarce countries, entrepreneurship can be a low-cost, high-impact approach to economic development.

b) New entrepreneurial ventures promote competition, efficiency and productivity; contribute to economic flexibility; strengthen supply chain development; ensure an inclusive process of development; and act as role models for others to pursue an entrepreneurial career. They create new industries and firms to replace those that have run their course.

c) According to Bogdan Glavan, Prof. of Economics, Bucharest University, the social or public benefits arising from entrepreneurial actions are greater than the private gains.

d) Successful entrepreneurs are truly change agents in the sense that they discover opportunities for making surpluses, which inspire other entrepreneurs to learn the processes and replicate them. Many such Startups eventually grow into SMEs and participate more vigorously in the development of a region. When many such businesses come into being, new production methods, new markets and new forms of organizations follow.

e) Entrepreneurs promote capital formation by mobilizing the idle savings of the public besides, of course, employing their own as well as borrowed funds.

f) They promote balanced regional development. When they set up enterprises in less developed and backward areas, regional disparities are lessened.

g) Of course, new enterprises increase GDP and per capita incomes thereby improving citizens' standard of living.

h) The taxes they pay contribute to the country's income.

The underlying principle of the process of entrepreneurial initiatives leading to employment growth and overall economic expansion is that: When entrepreneurial businesses transform an invention/innovation into a new product, for which market could be created, there is limited immediate competition. There is, therefore, scope for charging a price high enough to generate high surpluses, which would fund rapid expansion.

A few small businesses in time grow into big businesses and they invest part of their wealth for the good of the people. Some of the best Universities in the US are sustained by endowments of enlightened, successful entrepreneurs. The best of entertainment and fine arts are promoted by the munificence of entrepreneurs. Any society will surely be a dull place without the passion, creativity, energy and commitment of entrepreneurs; remember how the dead hand of the State strangled the erstwhile hard-core communist countries. Even in India, the mindless bureaucratic controls have been stifling entrepreneurial initiatives in the past.

Particularly for developing and transition economies, entrepreneurial individuals are critical. They create and build high - growth enterprises which in turn create productive and decent jobs, solve problems, meet needs or supply products and services. They contribute to economic expansion and poverty deduction.

Entrepreneurship is an attractive option for marginalized groups (Scheduled Caste, Scheduled Tribes and Other Backward Communities) including women. After all, there are no entry barriers in terms of educational qualifications or age or any other attribute.

To conclude, the powerful role played by dynamic entrepreneurial small businesses in bringing about socio-economic advancement is clearly validated around the world. Besides the obvious contributions of creating new technologies, new products and new services that multiply our choices and enrich our lives, high growth Startups are the best generators of **new jobs, jobs that did not previously exist**. In fact, economic growth is determined by how far economic reforms help or hinder entrepreneurship, which explains the phenomenon of some countries becoming rich while others remaining poor.

The Kauffman Foundation in its 2011 Thoughtbook had this to say about entrepreneurship: *"More than any time in history, entrepreneurship appears to be taking its rightful place on the world stage as central to any nation's efforts to build its economy."*

2.2 THE POWER AND PROMISE OF ENTREPRENEURIAL MSMEs

"At a time when many societies confront extremism, unemployment and slow economic growth , entrepreneurship holds out the promise of opportunity, prosperity and security," Barack Obama, President of the USA

Micro, Small and Medium Enterprises (MSMEs) are the seedbed of entrepreneurship, driven by innovation and creativity.

A relatively small group of entrepreneurial small businesses propel the economy forward even in highly developed countries; they have a disproportionate share of new jobs created and are estimated to account for about 50% of the difference in economic growth rates among industrial nations.

Companies that are 5 years old or younger, driven by innovation and, of course, being source of new jobs, have always been at the heart of US economic success.

Small firms had a higher percentage of patents per employee than larger firms, as per the analysis of US Small Business Administration. They are proven innovators and are the driving force behind a number of technological breakthroughs.

Kauffman Foundation estimates that 67% of all innovations and 95% of all radical innovations since World War II originated from entrepreneurial firms mostly based in the US: Voice Mail, telegraph, mobile phone, Internet shopping, digital entertainment, airplanes, air-conditioning, helicopter, computers (mainframe, personal and mini) and most software, safety razors, the car etc. Of course, most entrepreneurial firms fail but there are a few which grow to have the impact of companies like Ford, GM, IBM, Microsoft, Intel, Apple, Google or Facebook.

MSMEs are often close at hand, addressing issues and serving customers that are not always attractive to large enterprises.

The bureaucracy is slim; those performing the work and those supervising are close to each other without causing communication gaps. Being essentially a flat organization, free of traditional hierarchical structures, entrepreneurial MSMEs help foster continuous individual as well as collective learning.

As the global economy continues to wobble, the importance of entrepreneurial Startups in creating new jobs around the globe is greater than ever before. They are nimble and agile and more willing to innovate and pursue opportunities more vigorously than their larger, well-established competitors. They can often respond quickly and flexibly to customer needs. Their size and structure often allow them the flexibility to weather adverse economic conditions.

Notwithstanding the above relative strengths of small enterprises, there is evidence to demonstrate that workers at bigger firms are more productive than those at smaller firms. The large-scale operations allow large firms to introduce a range of productivity-enhancing processes. But then, the overall benefits that small enterprises deliver more than compensate for the lower worker productivity.

The importance of MSMEs in the economies of EU countries could be realized from the following statistics:

a) In terms of number of enterprises, MSMEs account for as much as 99.8% of enterprises.

b) MSMEs generate close to two-thirds of the total employment in EU.

c) In terms of Value addition at Factor costs, they account for 57.6% of all enterprises.

d) The Annual Report on European MSMEs, 2012–13 states, "Providing the right conditions in which MSMEs can flourish is paramount for ensuring a sustained recovery and achieving prosperity for all EU citizens".

In OECD countries, MSMEs account for over 95% of all firms, 60–70% of employment and 55% of GDP; they create most of **new** jobs.

In Canada, 98% of businesses are small and medium-sized.

The share of MSMEs in the work force and GDP is much higher in low-income countries.

The US scene

Small businesses (less than 500 employees) account for:

a) 99.7% of all employers
b) Half of the non-farm output
c) Half of all Americans not working for Govt.
d) Creating 60–80% of net new jobs annually
e) 97% of exporters
f) About 85% of the Forbes 400 wealthiest individuals, who20 were self-made entrepreneurs.
g) Kauffman Foundation claims, "**Without Startups, there would be no net job creation in the USA... Small entrepreneurial firms have been the catalyst for economic growth and America's secret economic weapon.**"

The Indian scene

Small business is big business in India and is the economic foundation of the country. The non-corporate small business sector is one of the largest disaggregated business ecosystems in the world sustaining around 500 mln. lives (Source: MUDRA Bank)

The sector comprises the widest possible range of activities including small manufacturing units, shopkeepers, fruits/vegetable vendors, truck and taxi operators, food-service units, repair shops, machine operators, small industries, artisans, food processors and street vendors. MSMEs account for:

a) Over 95% of all industrial units
b) 37% of manufacturing output, 46% exports and 40% industrial employment (**the prime driver of new employment**)
c) Nearly 38% of GDP (of which manufacturing shares 7.0% and services 31.0%) as per the 4th MSME Census (2013–14).
d) Almost 80% of the jobs, including those in the non-industrial sector
e) Employment of over 110 million persons in the estimated 51 million units (over 90% of them being in the unorganized sector)

with the market value of fixed assets of about Rs. 14,000 billion and gross output of over Rs. 18,000 billion.

f) The annual growth rate of the sector was a robust 18.74% during 2015–16.

Micro enterprises of self-employed entrepreneurs are the bedrock of the unorganized, informal sector which accounts for an overwhelming share of gross value added and employment in the total MSMEs segment. Unregistered micro enterprises account for close to 95% of the MSMEs sector. In fact, this sector offers the greatest opportunity both for self-employment as well as for jobs outside the agricultural sector. The National Entrepreneurship Policy document states that non-farm unorganized sector contributes close to 90% of the gross value added and nearly 98% of employment in the MSMEs sector.

Prof. R. Vaidyanathan, a leading academic and financial expert, has done some clever number-crunching to demonstrate the exceptionally high contribution being made by the unincorporated or non-corporate sector comprising partnership and proprietorship firms and self-employed persons (*INDIA UNINC*, 2014, Westland Ltd.):

This sector is the **largest contributor to national income, savings** (40% as opposed to 15% by the corporate sector) and **investment** (50% of gross domestic capital formation), **both direct and indirect taxes, credit markets, employment** and **foreign exchange earnings**.

The Report of the Working Group of the Govt. of India on MSMEs argues that the contribution of the sector is more profound than these broad numbers would suggest:

a) MSME sector creates employment at a lower cost per unit of capital.

b) It helps in the industrialization of rural and backward areas, and, hence, it minimizes imbalances in regional development.

c) MSMEs assure more equitable distribution of income and wealth.

d) Environmental impact of a larger number of small units tends to be less harmful than a smaller number of large units.

MSMEs complement large industries as ancillary units. They feed large local/international value chains and domestic consumer markets.

An interesting recent development has been the sharp growth of female entrepreneurship and business ownership, mostly household-based enterprises. Employment in the female-owned manufacturing businesses in India has increased significantly. A World Bank Policy Research Paper links this phenomenon to the empowerment of women brought about by legislations which reserved a minimum number of seats for women in elected public bodies at the village, municipality, State and national levels.

Kudumbasree (meaning prosperity of family), a Society, has leveraged the entrepreneurial talents of ordinary women in Kerala. It has become Asia's largest women's enterprise involving 4.0 mln. female participants, creating an incredibly large range of businesses from artisan shops to She taxis. The Society has won many awards including the UN's "We the people" award.

Entrepreneurial small businesses are also critical to address some of India's chronic developmental issues: Endemic poverty, affordable health care, clean water and sanitation, post-harvest agricultural processing etc.

In fact, in a capital-scarce, labour-surplus economy like India, the role of MSMEs in contributing to the national objective of inclusive growth with equity cannot be overstated.

The waxing and waning of Indian e-commerce Startups

India has been in the midst of an unprecedented entrepreneurial upsurge in the space of e-commerce the like of which the country has never experienced before. An ASSOCHAM – Forester study forecasts that India's e-commerce sector will touch US $120 bln. by 2020 from $30 bln. at the end of the financial year 2015–16. Goldman Sachs has estimated that the country's e-commerce market will grow to $300 billion by 2030.

This growth will be driven by young demographic profile, rising Internet penetration and relatively stronger economic performance. The major online hits are branded apparel, accessories, jewellery, gifts and footwear.

India's Internet user base is 400 mln. in 2016. Of course, the number of active users is much smaller and those who make purchases online are much, much smaller.

Although Indian online sales are the fastest growing market globally (51% per annum compared to 18% in China, 11% in Japan and 10% in South Korea), it's present base is lower than China or Japan.

Availability of funding, mentors, a market ready for new products and, of course, an emerging group of young entrepreneurs willing to take the plunge explain the growth of e-commerce sector in India.

A rain of money has been falling on young e-commerce/consumer Internet entities, elevating their valuations sky-high. (Current valuations reflect potential return multiple - number of times the returns can multiply - on an investment in, say, 5–6 years as determined by Venture Capitalists who are not particularly concerned about the losses currently being incurred by such entities).

Securities and Exchange Board of India has eased mandatory disclosure rules for Internet companies planning Initial Public Offering. Such a step will simultaneously help PE investors, which have invested billions in e-commerce entities, to exit their portfolio companies when their shares get listed.

Many e-commerce firms have unsustainable business models; the more products they sell, the more money they lose. These firms capture market share from offline retailers and each other by selling at low prices. These prices do not fully incorporate the marketing and logistics costs.

We may recall the dot-com bubble of late 90s when firms pursued 'revenue-now-profit-later' model. Promise of Indian Internet has been over-hyped in the recent past and record amount of capital was raised. Signs of irrational exuberance are surely visible.

Within the first four months of 2016, several e-commerce Startups either shut down or scaled back operations. Many national and international financial players have downgraded the valuations of some of the high-flyers in the sector. For instance, this year (2016) so far e-commerce giant Flipkart was devalued twice; HSBC slashed Zomato's billion-dollar valuation in half. Both are struggling to raise cash at their current valuations.

Independent observers believe that Indian e-commerce space may see a shakeout in the next 3 years or so. Top 10 to 20% of the Startups can transform themselves into big companies. Most others run the risk of falling by the wayside. Even big players like Flipkart and Snapdeal have to improve their technologies and processes to maintain their growth momentum.

There is a greater awareness now than ever before that Startups, instead of chasing the mirage of valuation, must build real businesses that generate revenue and surplus. They are, therefore, to be lean, focused and efficient.

Turbocharged leading players include:

a) 8-year old **Flipkart** is India's most valuable Startup with an estimated valuation of $15 billion (the first e-commerce Unicorn – a company whose valuation exceeds $1 billion before Public Issue) This e-commerce player provides online shopping options for a variety of products like books, mobile phones, digital cameras, laptops, watches and clothing at the best price in India.

b) **Snapdeal** is India's largest online shopping site.

c) **Zomato**, a restaurant search platform, with operations in UAE, New Zealand, Poland, Turkey, the Philippines and USA besides India.

d) **OLA Cabs**, India's largest taxi aggregator.

e) **Paytm**, an e-commerce website offers mobile recharging, bill payment and e-commerce with products similar to businesses such as Flipkart, Amazon.com and Snapdeal, and booking bus travel.

f) **Shopclues**, the latest Indian Unicorn, is an online bazaar that sells anything from unboxed mobile phones to cow dung!

The notable feature is that for the 50 million - strong MSMEs in the country, the e-commerce platform is giving a vast marketing channel to reach out to millions of customers within and outside the country at a much lower cost than conventional channels.

India's tech Startups are sizzling

India has emerged as the 3rd largest and the world's fastest growing tech Startup hub in the world estimated at 4200 in 2015, after US (47,000) and UK (4500). Such tech Startups are expected to grow to 11,500 by 2020; the employment in these Startups to expand to 250,000 from 75,000 at present.

(In terms of total number of Startups, tech and non-tech, India figures among the five largest hosts in the world along with China, 10,000 each)

NASSCOM's (National Association of Software and Service Companies, India) updated estimates/insights relating to Startups in the ICT sector:

a) Four Startups emerge per day. Total number was in excess of 4200 by end 2015, most of them e-commerce and consumer services entities, mobile firms and aggregators.

b) Number of accelerators and incubators grew 40% in 2015 over 2014 to 110.

c) India has emerged as the youngest Startup country with average age of founders at 28.

d) India is expected to witness about $6.5 billion funding in Startups in 2015. Global investors look at India, world's 3rd largest Startup hub, creating products and solutions for the domestic market; such products are eminently suitable for customers in other emerging markets in Asia, Africa and Latin America.

e) Rapidly evolving entrepreneurial landscape; millions of consumers with access to internet willing to spend on personal goods, healthcare and entertainment; and expanding industry-specific technical infrastructure, especially Incubators and Accelerators (over 80 now), providing Seed-stage support and a 4-fold increase in access to capital through VCs and Angel Investments and Seed funding explain this growth story. However, valuations of the Indian Startups, barring a few e-commerce entities, are not as high as those in the US, Israel or China. For most of the Tech Startups, the pot of gold at the end of the rainbow is afar because:

f) Only very, very few have been delivering strong returns so far
   i. Inadequately developed mergers and acquisitions market
   ii. IPOs (Initial Public Offering) for the majority being a distant dream

The smartly designed, 2-year old initiative, **NASSCOM 10,000 Startups**, has yielded excellent results. Innovative tech Startups in the space of Web, Mobile, Software, Internet of Things etc. are offered a robust portfolio of services in the different stages - ideation, early stage and growth stage. The programme is aimed at building entrepreneurial capabilities and fostering entrepreneurship. The range of support includes:

a) Evangelizing and mentoring Incubation at leading Incubators in India along with co-working space at affordable cost.
b) Funding ranging from Rs. 2.5 million to Rs. 20 million.
c) Free Startup kit worth Rs.1 million from Microsoft, AWS and Google.
d) Undertaking overseas Startup delegations to Silicon Valley, Israel, Hong Kong and parts of Europe to showcase India's most innovative tech Startups building world-class products.
e) Creating the NASSCOM Technology Startup Registry that will act as a repository of India's technology Startups, a discovery platform for investors, enterprises, media and Government authorities.
f) Launching a skill initiative to increase talent pool of skills for tech Startups job market.

During the first two phases of the programme, 7000 Startups responded to the initiative of which 529 were short-listed and 125+ startups have got the support of the programme.

IBM is deepening its association with early-stage companies in India, given the country's fertile and rapidly evolving technology ecosystem and abundant quality talents. IBM has launched its first public cloud data centre in India in Oct 2015. IBM has also launched, in partnership with NASSCOM, an online hub called Techstartup.in which will allow Startups, investors and venture capitalists to network with each other as part of a drive to help grow the cloud marketing in India.

MSMEs - the engines of economic growth and social stability

(Summarized from SEAF's 2011 Development Impact Report)

MSMEs create most new jobs. Most MSMEs tend to be located in rural and semi-urban centers employing semi-skilled or unskilled local workers who would otherwise fall into the ranks of the poor. In fact, they generally hire relatively poor people. (Majority of over 15 million young people joining the labour market per year in the next decade in India will belong to this category).

This is a mutually reinforcing process: Most such workers spend a larger share of their income on products produced by less skilled workers. Such small businesses establish more supply links with local MSMEs. When employees leave micro-enterprises to join SMEs, their wage incomes rise and become steady making it easier to plan for the long-term welfare of their families. The above process triggers the growth of more SMEs, releasing a positive multiplier effect.

MSMEs:

a) Introduce business methods, products and services that help restructure weak rural economies.

b) Often satisfy the unmet demand in their local markets; try and succeed in making available new, high quality and competitively priced products and services thereby enhancing the quality of life of local consumers.

c) Help spread the benefits of economic growth by forming dynamic supply-chain linkages between small-scale producers and growing urban, national and export markets. They also link, in the reverse direction, large urban businesses with mass consumer markets in the remote areas.

d) Improve the lives of employees. Employees are provided skills training, thereby helping them acquire valuable skills - a passport out of poverty.

e) Impact positively on local producers of complementary goods and services.

f) Contribute to the tax revenue of the local, state and national Governments. (Many micro enterprises, of course, may belong to the Informal Sector and may not be paying any taxes.)

> Based on SEAF's analysis, the multiplier effect or total economic impact of MSMEs on their local economies is estimated at an additional $13 for every $ invested.

WHAT IS GOOD FOR MSMEs IS GOOD FOR INDIA!

3
The Entrepreneur: An Enigma Wrapped In A Mystery

"Anybody can see a seed in an apple, the wise person sees an apple in a seed"
—**An African proverb**

"Some look at things and ask 'why'? Others look at things and ask 'why not'?'... The reasonable man adapts himself to the world; the unreasonable one persists in trying to adapt the world to him. Therefore, all progress depends on the unreasonable man."
—**George Bernard Shaw**

"Millions saw the apple fall but Newton was the one to ask why."
—**Bernard M. Baruch**

3.1 THE WORLD OF ENTREPRENEURS

The entrepreneurial journey from the initial intuition to the launch of the product and, of course, managing the enterprise thereafter is extremely tortuous.

Jeff Haden, a prominent contributor to Inc.com, wrote, *"From a rational point of view, starting a business is crazy. The failure rate is high, the emotional toll is high and the likelihood of having to work extremely hard for potentially little reward is incredibly high."*

According to the Schumpeter column in The Economist dated Sep 2014 (titled *Entrepreneurs Anonymous*), *"... first-time founders have the job security of zero-hour contract workers, and the money worries of chronic gamblers and the social life of hermits."*

The world of an entrepreneur is characterized by:

a) Struggling with issues of gaining legitimacy and support among many stakeholders including partners, investors and banks, suppliers, employees and customers.

b) Unimaginable uncertainties, ambiguities and complexities.

c) Having to do everything under pressure and the consequent stress both for the entrepreneur and his family; being on an emotional roller coaster.

d) Coping with loneliness; the scariness of being the only one responsible for the success or failure of the business; being responsible for the welfare of a given group of people.

e) Learning by doing, copying, making things up, problem solving.

f) Working long hours: 70–80 hours per week not being uncommon. ("*An entrepreneur is a self-employed person working 16 hours a day to avoid working 8 hours a day for someone else!*")

g) Threat of business failure: Possibility of losing one's money and that of others, long-term indebtedness.

h) Having the choices of 'life' and 'death', mostly the latter!

Thomas L. Friedman in his book, *The World is Flat*, quotes the following African proverb to highlight, somewhat dramatically, the struggle an entrepreneur goes through in an environment of uncertainties and chaos:

"Every morning in Africa, a gazelle wakes up. It knows it must run faster than the fastest lion or it will be killed. Every morning a lion wakes up. It knows it must outrun the slowest gazelle or it will starve to death. It doesn't matter whether you are a lion or gazelle. When the sun comes up, you better start running."

What drives a rational person to choose a path leading to such a demanding, imperfect, messy and risky world? We surely are not claiming that we are in the process of discovering a 'general theory' to explain the riddle. All that we are attempting is to get a sense of:

a) The entrepreneur and his traits.

b) Why he does what he does.

c) Why some people but not others choose the entrepreneurial career; why some people but not others recognize opportunities for new products that can be profitably exploited.

d) Why some entrepreneurs are more successful than others. Why some entrepreneurial ventures are successful over the long-term while others fail after a promising start.

e) Why entrepreneurship flourishes in some regions and stagnate in other places. How and why a

f) significantly large proportion (when weighted to the total population) of Marwaris, Sindhis, Gujaratis or Punjabis from India has been successful entrepreneurs within and outside India.

Admittedly, answers to some of these and similar questions in the sphere of entrepreneurship are not easy to come by.

3.2 DEFINING AN ENTREPRENEUR

An entrepreneur is when "persistence, passion and purpose collide."

There is no accepted definition or model of what the entrepreneur is or does. Entrepreneurs are not a homogenized group; they come in a wide variety of shapes and sizes. The literature is full of criteria ranging from creativity and innovation to the identification and exploitation of an opportunity or starting a new business where there was none before.

An entrepreneur is one who discovers a customer need and exploits the opportunity by meeting the need with a new product in creative ways, before someone else does. Of course, an entrepreneur can also enter an existing market and beat the competition by offering a better product in terms of quality, functionality, price, mode of distribution and promotion, service level, packaging etc.

OECD defines entrepreneurs as *"those persons (business owners) who seek to generate value through the creation or expansion of economic activity by identifying and exploiting new products, processes or markets."*

UNCTAD's definition of entrepreneur: *"An entrepreneur is an individual who identifies opportunities in the market place, allocates resources and creates value."*

Entrepreneur is "... *somebody who offers an innovative solution to a (frequently unrecognized) problem*" - The Economist, March 14, 2009

An entrepreneur can be an individual, an entrepreneurial team or even an entrepreneurial organization. He may create his own unique business or work as a member of a team, as in multi-level marketing.

The term 'entrepreneur' derives from two etymologically related Latin words meaning one who penetrates and transgresses established boundaries and seizes the opportunities otherwise overlooked by others.

The French verb *"entreprendre"* - to undertake, to attempt, to adventure, to try - is considered the earliest use of the term. Many French authors referred to the term in connection with brutal war-like activities; others referred to an entrepreneur as someone who is tough and prepared to risk his own life and future.

Potential promoters of enterprises represent different demographic and professional background and, of course, with the widest possible range of personality characteristics:

a) An inventor having a product idea.

b) An innovator who has developed a new product. (Inventors/Innovators are not necessarily great business people. Johannes Gutenberg, who invented the world-altering printing technology, died a pauper)

c) An entrepreneur who wants to create a business.

d) A professional manager who wants to create a business.

e) An unemployed person who wants to create a job for himself.

A unique characteristic of an entrepreneur is that he reads situations differently from others. When most people see risks, he sees opportunities. He can overcome obstacles that would stop most people. He sees failure as a temporary setback, an investment in learning to do better next time.

Most people develop analysis-paralysis, never pulling the trigger; entrepreneurs analyze to a point, then they jump in.

At heart, an entrepreneur is a kind of "speculator". After all, he deals with an uncertain future. But he does attempt anticipating and meeting the needs of customers, who today may not know his product, and offering a solution to a specific problem they face, better than the competition.

Indeed, such consumers may even have to be "discovered". How good he is at anticipating the future outcomes of decisions he takes today will determine his success or failure.

Entrepreneurs seem to be more religious than others. The pressure of starting and managing a business appears to heighten their spiritual leanings. Could it be that people with greater faith in God are more willing to take risks? As per an estimate about 9 out of 10 entrepreneurs are affiliated with some religion, they pray more and are more likely to believe in an engaged, responsive God who takes a personal interest in them.

To rephrase a smart–aleck quote of Peter McArthur (1901) reproduced in *How to Succeed in Business*:

A successful entrepreneur is an amalgam of three people -
A dreamer, a doer and a son-of-a-bitch (not necessarily in that order!)

3.2.1 Entrepreneur Vs Small Business Owner

All entrepreneurs are business people, but not all business people are entrepreneurs. An entrepreneur is a business-minded person who constantly scans the environment looking for changes that can provide opportunities for creating new growth-oriented businesses.

Small businesses deal with known and established products and services. Entrepreneurial ventures are for new innovative offerings. Small businesses deal with known risks; entrepreneurial ventures take on opportunities with lots of unknown risks.

Entrepreneurial ventures scale fast, look for high profitability impacting economies and communities. Small businesses remain confined to their own domain and group.

3.3 ENTREPRENEUR - THE RENAISSANCE MAN

There has been an attempt at mythologizing the entrepreneur as *"hero/ heroine, a warrior, and a maverick."* Entrepreneurs have a larger than life image. They dream big and their motives are complex, beyond making money or avoiding loss or building an organization.

Entrepreneurial ability is utterly scarce; this scarcity endows it with immense prestige and value. There is the heroic view of the entrepreneur: Entrepreneurship is so difficult to attain, it is only for an exceptional few.

According to Amar Bhidé, author of *The Origin and Evolution of New Businesses*, "... it takes a really extraordinary individual to build a promising company - extraordinary in terms of someone who has an almost maniacal level of ambition. Not just an ambition to make a comfortable living, to make a few million dollars, but someone who wants to leave a significant mark on the world."

Joseph Schumpeter, the celebrated economist who plumbed the depths of entrepreneurship more than the most, presented a vision of daring individual entrepreneurs possessed of *"supernatural qualities of intellect and will"*.

Shorn of the romanticism, the notion of a Hercules building a corporate colossus may seem more a myth than reality.

a) Entrepreneurship is essentially a collective effort, seldom a solitary activity. In contrast to popular myths, successful entrepreneurs actively associate others to be part of their team as co-founders, employees, investors, advisors or unpaid helpers.

b) One person may come to be recognized as "the innovator" but it always takes a team of competent people to make any venture work. Some of the most successful tech enterprises have been the outcome of collaborative efforts: Steve Jobs & Steve Wozniak (Apple), Sergei Brin & Larry Page (Google), David Filo & Jerry Young (Yahoo!) Pierre Omidyar & Jeffrey Skoll (eBay) and N.R. Narayana Murthy, Nandan Nilekani, Shibulal, Kris Gopalakrishnan and other co-founders of Infosys in India.

c) Steve Hogan, who runs a Startup turn-around consulting entity, confidently states that enterprises

d) founded by one person, without partners, are most likely to fail. Having co-founders helps confront some of the typical problems Startups face.

Entrepreneurial successes are, therefore, the outcome of a variety of factors including competencies of those who work in an enterprise. Of course, our Renaissance Man did create the environment to inspire his partners and employees to give of their best.

3.4 IS AN ENTREPRENEUR BORN OR MADE?

Is an entrepreneur a product of 'nature' or 'nurture'? Are entrepreneurial traits a part of the genetic make-up of a person (leading him to seek particular opportunities) or are such qualities acquired or learned?

Here, we are trying to say an entrepreneur is born, only to devalue the argument later!

Many analysts believe that most entrepreneurs are born; entrepreneurial instinct is part of their nature. The argument is that there appears to be a high degree of commonality of specific traits among entrepreneurs, which are, in fact, somewhat subliminal and psychologically inspired.

It is irrefutable that being an entrepreneur is not for everyone. After all, only a tiny proportion of the population in any society at any time could live with the stress, risks and responsibilities of having large (or even small) number of persons' lives depending on the decisions one takes. Most people tend to settle for safer or less demanding career options.

Ambition explains why some are obsessed with the need to get ahead, to achieve whereas most others are content to accept whatever life brings. Ambition is an essential trait to have to be successful in any field, particularly when taking on entrepreneurial challenges, and is described as a product of evolution.

An article in the TIME magazine on the science of ambition states that, "... *two of the biggest influences on your level of ambition are the family that produced you and the culture that produced your family.*"

In fact, the socio-cultural background of the entrepreneur and his family appears to play a role in moulding a successful entrepreneur. In India, specific communities (Marwaris and Chettiars, for example) and regions (Punjab and Gujarat) have nurtured disproportionately large number (relative to their size in the general population) of successful entrepreneurs.

Every entrepreneur is surely a blend of traits, skills and strengths. The traits represent the psychological capital of the entrepreneur; they are seemingly more behavioural than skill-related or education-based. When we deal with behavioural sciences - Psychology, Cognitive Science etc. - we may remind ourselves that they are not as precise as pure sciences.

According to an oft-quoted researcher, Sara D. Saraswathy, all entrepreneurs begin with three sets of 'resources' - *"with these resources, the entrepreneurs dream, innovate and execute"*:

a) Who they are: their traits, tastes and abilities,

b) What they know: their education, training, experience and expertise,

c) Whom they know: their social and professional network.

(Refer to discussion on entrepreneurial traits at 3.6 and on teaching entrepreneurship at 4.5 to learn more.)

3.5. CLASSIFYING ENTREPRENEURS

Steve Bank of Kauffman Foundation identified four distinct organizational paths for entrepreneurs:

a) Small businesses most of which tend to remain small. In countries like India, most are in the informal (non-tax paying) sector.

b) Scalable Startups: A few promoted by exceptionally smart and driven entrepreneurs, which are born to grow. Microsoft, Apple, Facebook, Google etc. are examples of high-flying, technology-oriented companies.

c) Large companies, which are driven by the motto "innovate or evaporate". Such companies have extensive R&D programmes that keep creating new products and processes that are leveraged for global leadership. GEC, Sony, Toyota, Siemens are examples.

d) There is the entrepreneurial employee activity, related to intrapreneurship - employees of an existing company pursuing entrepreneurial activities with the support of the management.

e) Not-for-profit entities which want to make an impact or a difference. They focus on specific societal concerns and measure their success in terms of social goals rather than profit. The value of the local society is put before the value of the individual leading those initiatives. They are agents of change rather than profit-seeking enterprises.

An outstanding case of not-profit ventures is the Sammaan Foundation founded by Irfan Alam. An alumnus of one of India's top Business Schools, Alam created an example of social entrepreneurship. Alam redesigned the humble rickshaw, the ubiquitous and inexpensive urban means of transport in some of the least developed regions in the country, making it much lighter than the traditional ones thereby making it easier to pedal and more comfortable to ride in. He invented a business model that is a win-win formula for the rickshaw pullers, the banks that fund the cost of the rickshaw and the Foundation which co-ordinates all the activities.

Opportunity-driven vs. Necessity-driven

a) Opportunity-driven entrepreneurs are those having the need for achievement (pull motivation), desire to be independent and, above all, want to take advantage of an opportunity.

b) Necessity-driven (push motivation) entrepreneurs take to self-employment not because they identified new market opportunities or innovative ideas but merely because of risk of unemployment, family pressures, dissatisfaction with the present occupation or absence of better choices of work. Many of such enterprises tend to be low-skill, small-scale subsistence activities.

A new firm based on an innovative idea to create an innovative product to meet a customer need or solve a customer problem in new ways will have a higher chance of a better post-entry performance than a new firm started on the basis of a purely 'defensive' motivation such as the fear of becoming unemployed.

Accidental vs. Purposeful Entrepreneurs

This classification distinguishes the manner in which they begin building the businesses.

Characteristics of Accidental Entrepreneurs:

a) Building a small business for a product to meet a very specific need

b) Staying relatively small, within the founder's comfort zone

c) Most of them fail when they either can't or won't make the transition to professional management to benefit from proven processes of planning, analyzing alternative options, executing against pre-set norms, evaluating the outcomes etc.

Characteristics of Purposeful Entrepreneurs:

a) They begin with a vision of greatness, inspired by size and scale
b) They love business for business sake - as the highest expression of the most complex strategic games that humans play.
c) They plan to win: Get the right team, raise capital, execute quickly.
d) They have the courage, confidence and audacity to embrace the backbreaking effort required to create an enterprise from nothing.

Replicative vs. Innovative

a) Replicative (or imitative) entrepreneurs open businesses of standard variety, say, retail outlets.
b) Innovative entrepreneurs are concerned with new products, new processes, new markets or new ways of putting innovation to work for the society. These entrepreneurs are the drivers of long-term economic growth because they translate inventions into commercially successful products and services.

Formal vs. Informal

a) Formal: A firm registered with the appropriate government agency operating in a formal (taxable) sector.
b) Informal: They operate largely outside state regulatory system and go unmonitored despite their significant contribution to poverty reduction and economic development. Millions in countries like India operate in informal sectors, engaged in legal activities. The downside of the operation of such enterprises includes worker exploitation, tax evasion and corruption. Some of them become formal enterprises once they grow and realize the benefits from doing so.

3.6 UNDERSTANDING ENTREPRENEURIAL TRAITS

"You will be the most important reason that your business succeeds or fails"
- Michael D. Zeiders, *Entrepreneurship - The Art of Succeeding in Business*

What does it take to be an entrepreneur, and a successful one at that? Is there a commonality of entrepreneurial **characteristics** or **capabilities** or **pre-dispositions** or **a distinctive personality**

profile or an **entrepreneurial alertness** or **a sixth sense** that allows them to recognize opportunities and exploit them, which others miss?

As early as 1934, Joseph Schumpeter pronounced: *"The entrepreneur uses his personality and nothing but his personality."*

Entrepreneurs are considered to have a unique set of stable, inherent and enduring personality characteristics - permanent and remain consistent across time and context. These traits are conceived to be inborn and a matter of personality. Those who believe in the traits theory assume that such traits can neither be learned nor developed through education and training or even professional experience. In fact, no one really knows if one is an entrepreneur until he becomes one!

THE UNENDING SEARCH FOR THE TRAITS

Attempts at identifying and defining entrepreneurial traits have been the most tantalizing aspect of the study of entrepreneurship. The search for 'entrepreneurial personality' has been just about as fascinating as the search for the Himalayan Snowman or Loch Ness Monster! There have, in fact, been as many explorations into this area (and, therefore, interpretations) as there are researchers, analysts and authors.

McClelland's Cross Cultural Competencies (1987)

The enquiries of David McClelland into the inter-relatedness of achievement motivation, the role of the entrepreneur and economic development had identified three sets of traits of successful entrepreneurs regardless of country and type of business:

1. **Proactiveness**
    a) Initiative: Does things before being asked or forced to by events.
    b) Assertiveness: Confronts problems with others directly; tells others what they have to do.
2. **Achievement Orientation**
    a) Sees and acts on opportunities: Seizes unusual opportunities, obtains financing, land, workspace, or assistance.

b) Efficiency orientation: Looks for or finds ways to do things faster or at less cost.

c) Concern for high quality of work: States a desire to produce or sell a top or better quality product or service.

d) Systematic planning: Breaks a large task down into subtasks or sub goals, anticipates obstacles, and evaluates alternatives.

e) Monitoring: Develops or uses procedures to ensure that work is completed or that work meets standards of quality.

3. Commitment to Others

a) Commitment to work contract: Makes a personal sacrifice or expends extraordinary effort to complete a job, pitches in with workers or works in their place to get the job done

b) Recognizing the importance of business relationships: Acts to build rapport or friendly relationships with customers, sees interpersonal relationships as a fundamental business resource, places long-term goal over short-term gain.

A Hubris Theory of Entrepreneurship

Mathew Hayward, Dean Shepherd and Dale Griffin in their 2006 paper in the Management Science Journal argue that over-confidence provides founders with the audacity to promote very challenging projects driven by the conviction that they will be able to pull them off. Over-confidence helps the founders feel good about starting and achieving what they might not have otherwise attempted.

Over-confidence makes the promoters optimists thereby over-estimating the chances of success. Although many such ventures may fail, societies around the world benefited enormously from highly confident players who achieved remarkable success from very challenging tasks. Unarguably, all leading successful entrepreneurs - Henry Ford, Steve Jobs, Bill Gates, or Dhirubhai Ambani of Reliance Group in India - created individual and societal prosperity.

Entrepreneur-friendly afflictions

The June 2012 Schumpeter column in The Economist quotes several studies/analysts, highlighting a number of mental oddities:

a) 35% of entrepreneurs surveyed by Julie Logan of the Cass Business School said they suffered from Dyslexia (compared to 10% of the population as a whole and 1% of professional managers). Dyslexia is a development disorder marked by difficulty in reading and spelling. Prominent Dyslexics include founders of Ford, GE, IBM and IKEA and more recent achievers like Charles Schwab (founder of a stock broking firm), Richard Branson (The Virgin Group), John Chambers (CISCO) and Steve Jobs (Apple). This malady explains how such entrepreneurs learn to delegate tasks early and tend to taking on activities that require few formal qualifications and demand little reading or writing.

b) Attention-deficit disorder (ADD) is another entrepreneur-friendly affliction; people with ADD are found to be six times more likely than average to promote own business. *"With the disorganization, procrastination, inability to focus and all other bad things that come with ADD, there also come creativity and the ability to take risks."* - Paul Orfalea, a serial entrepreneur.

c) Asperger's syndrome is another malady internet-based entrepreneurs could be diagnosed with. This syndrome denotes an obsessive interest in narrow subjects, a passion for numbers, patterns and machines. Mark Zuckerberg, of Facebook, reportedly has a touch of Asperger's.

3.6.1 A list of entrepreneurial traits

1. **Vision**: The ability to spot an opportunity and imagine something which others have not. They imagine another world and have the ability to communicate that vision to investors, customers and staff. They see the future before the future plays out.

2. **Insight/Intuition:** The most crucial, indefinable ingredient; the ability to see things in new ways; seeing something about an industry or market that others miss or fail to realize the potential of and finding a way to convert that knowledge into a strong market position.

3. **A need to control/direct**: Although they have a need to create and achieve by having control over events, most entrepreneurs tend to seek achievement more than power. However, some may lose interest in the enterprise if they lose control.

4. **Self-confidence**: The belief that one can do what one sets out to do; unwavering belief in oneself; they are at their best in the face of adversity; they seldom recognize limits or boundaries. The proposition put forth by Vince Lombardi, the famous football player, coach, and executive, *"Life's battles don't always go to the stronger and faster man... The man who wins is the man who thinks he can."*, says it all.

5. **Internal Locus of Control/Self-nurturing/Self-efficacy**: Don't believe in luck; they believe that success or failure lies within one's personal control; self-motivated; an unwavering and total belief in themselves and never allow anyone or anything to dispel that belief.

6. **Need to succeed**: A persistent, restless, almost obsessive striving to succeed no matter what it takes; success to be defined in terms of wealth, recognition, social status, fame or power; above all, realizing a cherished dream.

7. **Leadership**: Inspire the team

8. **Focus**: Rated as one of the most important factors contributing to business success (The image on the cover of this book represents "Focus, Focus, Focus"). Focus is all about determining what one's priority is at any point in time/time period - product, service, hiring, fund raising, sales or innovation - and focusing on that one thing. Focus also means knowing what is not important at any given point in time. They are self-directed and self-disciplined, sticking to a schedule and a set of deadlines. They are action-oriented and focus on execution; success is the *"exceptional execution of an ordinary idea."*

9. **Risk-taking:** Tolerant of uncertainty/risks/ambiguity/adversity; willingness to leave one's comfort zone; the ability to take reasoned chances and accept failure as a learning opportunity; ability to take calculated risks, when there is uncertainty of the outcome of resources committed today; can anticipate business risks with a reasonable degree of accuracy. It means having the courage to expose oneself to possible losses, even bankruptcy and humiliation.

10. **Sense of urgency**: Time-conscious; will avoid wasting time on non-productive activities
11. **Need for autonomy and decisiveness**
12. **Competitive**: Willingness to test oneself against others, even the smartest.
13. **Realistic outlook**: Smart enough to know their limitations and ready to listen to experts.
14. **Rule breaking**: Entrepreneurs defy conventional wisdom. In fact, merely starting a business breaks the rule. Because only a very tiny proportion of the population becomes entrepreneurs.
15. **Emotional stability**: Immunity to stress, being calm, keeping one's cool amidst crisis.
16. **Emotional intelligence**: They can read people well; have an intuition about what will fly.
17. **Multi-tasking:** Switching contexts rapidly; chasing several things at one time (Not particularly desirable a trait because it spells lack of focus).
18. **Hiring ability**: Select the right people; picking the right advisors.
19. **Optimism/Hope:** Optimism means generalized positive outcome expectancy; they tend to be more optimistic than others. Hope gives them the ability to think up multiple routes through which one's goals may be achieved.
20. **Initiative**
21. **Creativity, inventiveness and innovation:**
    a) The ability to think up many possible outcomes and to proactively create the one most appropriate to a given context;
    b) Having original ideas and insights which are translated into products which touch human lives positively;
    c) Able to make connections between seemingly unrelated events or situations or things. They take old ideas or business models and improve them to make them attractive to the customers.
    d) Opportunistic imagination; out-of- the-box thinking;

e) Reframe the problem, breaking down into its components and reassemble them in a different way.
f) According to Dr. Ed McMullan, Professor of Innovation and Entrepreneurship, University of Calgary, creativity of the lead promoter is the only scientific predictor of entrepreneurial success. Such assertions need to be taken with some caution. *"Creativity is hard enough to sustain for individuals, let alone organizations. Business history is littered with the corpses of corporate Icaruses that rose heavenwards on the wings of creativity only to plunge to the ground"* - Schumpeter column, The Economist, June 2010.
g) The problem with the concept of creativity, however, is how one determines/measures how much one has of it.

22. Tenacity:
a) Perseverance/persistence: Refusal to quit; never giving up hope, to keep on trying and try something different. The stubborn perseverance of entrepreneurs confront the conventional wisdom which may say can't, won't or shouldn't be done.
b) Resilience: Bounces back from adversity; adapts to changing requirements; ability to deal with failures and learn from them.
c) Determination
d) Commitment

23. Discipline: One quality that no entrepreneur can do without.

24. Aggressive/assertive/strong-willed

25. Drive: The commitment to work hard to achieve one's goals.

26. Passion: Work is their play, what drives them internally to succeed, create and continuously strive for better that keeps them up late into the night. They believe, at the core level, what they are doing is their destiny.
a) What inspires, energizes and drives successful entrepreneurs is the passion, enthusiasm or fire in the belly.
b) There can be a downside to this trait in some cases. "The same passions that drive them to make something from nothing also drive them to crush anybody who gets in their way." - Schumpeter column, The Economist, March 2010.

27. **Attention to detail**: Not missing the trees for the forest.

28. **Persuasive ability**: Given the fact that an individual enterprise is constantly buffeted by developments in the environment, the entrepreneur has to develop the skills to try to manage the environment at some level or other, in some measure or other.

29. **Higher-than-average street smarts**

30. **Flexibility**: Adjust, adapt, modify and re-define the ideas in response to changing environment.

31. **Networking skills and relationship building**: Building bridges and network chains. Businesses are driven by relationships; people do business with those they know, like and trust. Network effect enhances the entrepreneur's ability to discover opportunities, get resources and gain legitimacy.

32. **Communication skills**

33. **Decisive but open-minded**: Sometimes will act impulsively on gut feeling; will reverse one's opinion when new information surfaces.

34. **Curiosity**: Asking a lot of questions, curiosity triggers innovation.

35. **Being independent**: Being one's own boss.

36. **Organized**: Not necessarily on paper but in their heads; can capture, analyze and recall the required information; the ability to structure one's life, tasks and information.

37. **High level of energy and enthusiasm**

38. **A "Type D" person**: Desire coupled with Drive, Discipline and Determination

39. **Professional**: Not allowing oneself to be distracted by outside influence.

40. **Some are cunning, opportunistic and unsentimental**: *"I built this business by being a bastard; I run it by being a bastard. I'll always be a bastard."* - Charles Revson, Promoter of Revlon, the global player in the cosmetics industry.

41. Some are **loners**: Preferring a solitary work environment as opposed to teamwork; many enjoy individual sports like golf or tennis more than team sports.

42. **Ambition**: A determination to accomplish success in the chosen field; aggressive, self-seeking or self-centered.

43. **Irrationality**: Most of the new businesses fail; hence, a rational person may not want to take on such an activity. It is the seemingly irrational people, taking risks that do not quite make logical sense, who make our world a better place.

44. **Consummate learner**: A successful entrepreneur has to have the ability to predict or anticipate the future. This ability is acquired through higher order learning: Learning-to-learn-how-to-learn.

45. **Other traits**: Walter Kuemmerle, in the May 2002 HBR article *A Test for the Fainthearted*, talks about the following traits of successful entrepreneurs:

    a) They are comfortable stretching the rules; bend the rules to get what they need; whatever it takes to achieve their ends.

    b) They are prepared to make powerful enemies in the pursuit of opportunities.

    c) They have the patience to start small. All new businesses are essentially taking a chance. Starting small gives the promoter the opportunity to test and fine-tune the concept before the project is launched on a full scale.

    d) They are willing to change strategy quickly. Most every assumption one makes can undergo change in short notice.

    e) They know how to close a deal. *"... They know what they must give up and what they can get away with. Many decisions could make the difference between life and death of the enterprise!"*

NON-BELIEVERS' ARGUMENT

As Amar Bhidé put it, "*... There is no ideal profile. Entrepreneurs can be gregarious or taciturn, analytical or intuitive, cautious or daring.*"

If successful entrepreneurs share a set of common traits, is it possible to anticipate the likelihood of success of an enterprise if one can determine whether or not the given promoter of the project possesses such traits? We are on a somewhat slippery ground when we take this concept forward. Which traits have what impact and how predictive are their values? Even if we identify such traits, how do we measure them in the first place? Researchers are yet to discover powerful analytical tools to assess the traits entrepreneurs are supposed to have.

Let us look at the arguments of the non-believers in the traits theory:

1. The traits that lead to entrepreneurial success are nearly the same as those of top performers in most other disciplines: Persistence, hard work, intelligence and creativity.
2. Different entrepreneurs take different paths to success, each marked by unique challenges and equally unique opportunities.
3. There is no one-size-fits-all way to understand any group of people, let alone entrepreneurs. No two entrepreneurs are the same:
   a) Some are extroverts and some are introverts.
   b) Some have a family history of entrepreneurship whereas others do not.
   c) Some come from financially challenged backgrounds whereas others are rich to begin with.
   d) Some are young and some are old.
   e) Some are men and some are women.
   f) Some are gentle, caring and consensus-seeking whereas others are autocratic and ruthless.
   g) Some are highly educated and others are college dropouts. In fact, four of the greatest entrepreneurs of our generation, Michael Dell, Bill Gates, Steve Jobs and Mark Zuckerberg did not complete their college education.
   h) Some entrepreneurs who failed in one or many enterprises succeed later and others who achieved initial success failed when their enterprises reach a certain stage.

Based on the research of Ernst & Young, an international consulting group, Dr. Thomas Muller, (*Exceptional*, July-December 2011, Ernst & Young), a leading criminal psychologist, concluded that beyond a shared aptitude for handling risk and pressure, entrepreneurs are as individual as the rest of us. According to Dr. Muller, three of the successful entrepreneurs' defining characteristics reveal themselves in crisis:

1. The ability to withstand pressure beyond a point at which most people would compromise for the sake of security.
2. An appetite for risk
3. The ability to adapt quickly to new circumstances.

Israel has created exceptionally large number of successful entrepreneurs in the hi-tech area operating within the country or in the US. One of the contributory factors identified for this phenomenon is that most such entrepreneurs have had military background.

Janelle Hill, Cheryl Lawhorne and Don Philipott, in their book *Life After the Military: A Handbook for Transitioning Veterans* claim, "… *The skills and strengths arising from military experience such as leadership, organization and the ability to work under pressure lend themselves naturally to entrepreneurship*". This example seems to validate the argument that the characteristics of a successful entrepreneur are gained from experiences and lessons learned earlier.

Non-believers are for focusing on what entrepreneurs do rather than what they are. Several situational factors - forces external to the person - will have impact on the success or failure of an enterprise.

Personality traits are ancillary or supportive to the activity of the entrepreneur; the surroundings determine entrepreneurial behaviour. After all, entrepreneurs do not operate in a vacuum; they have to continuously respond to the environment they are part of. This process does transform the entrepreneurial behaviour thereby impacting his personality traits. The behavioural approach suggests that entrepreneurship can be taught.

BEHAVIOURAL TRAITS UNDER ASSAULT

During the past decade, personality characteristics or behavioural traits have been downgraded as they are found to be inadequate differentiators of successful entrepreneurs from non-entrepreneurs. Person-centric models of entrepreneurship are not being considered as a science any more by many analysts. **Cognitive skills** are now being considered better at explaining entrepreneurial uniqueness.

According to Thomas N. Duening, author of the book *Technology Entrepreneurship*, the way entrepreneurs think differentiates them from non-entrepreneurs. The cognitive skills unique to entrepreneurs are described as the following 'minds':

1. The Opportunity Recognizing Mind.
2. The Designing Mind: Design a new product or recognize such design novelty or design a solution to a consumers' problem.
3. The Risk Managing Mind: Entrepreneurs are adept at risk minimizing; bring risk to levels that are tolerable.
4. The Resilient Mind: *'Ability to survive and even thrive under conditions of turbulence, change… ability to absorb defeat or bad news without losing one's focus on goals and objectives'*.
5. The Effectuating Mind: Action-orientation; creating something of value and delivering it to customers.

As hinted at earlier, few postulates relating to entrepreneurship have long shelf life. Sooner or later, an avenger will emerge to wrestle the theory of cognitive skills to the ground!

The point is that merely having a bunch of traits which successful entrepreneurs apparently have or acquire does not make one an entrepreneur nor does it guarantee success. The irony, however, is that success is required to be generally accepted as an entrepreneur.

Malcolm Gladwell, (author of *Outliers: the Story of Success*), argues that:

a) Outstanding success in every field is a function of great dedication, talent and fortuitous/ accidental circumstances including socio-economic context into which someone was born.

b) Geniuses are made not born; cultures and not genes create them. Success is not the sole result of individual initiative.

c) Deliberate Practice is the name of the game; consistent, intelligent practice to improve performance, get feedback, then practice to improve performance. Few, if any, possess a natural gift for a certain activity. Hard work is necessary but not sufficient. Practice makes perfect.

But how do you practice business? Presenting, negotiating, analyzing financial statements etc. are doable. Making judgments and decisions based on inadequate information in an unpredictable environment is indeed tough.

THE SKILLS MOST SERIAL ENTREPRENEURS LACK

(An excerpt from Bill J. Bonnstetter's article on HBR Blog Network, Apr1, 2013)

Entrepreneurs are a unique group of people, but they behave in pattern. Research shows that most serial entrepreneurs display persuasion, leadership, personal accountability, goal orientation, and interpersonal skills. But in the same study, we also discovered a set of skills they do not possess.

After analyzing the data, we found four distinct skills lacking in most serial entrepreneurs:

a) **Empathy** *is one of the qualities serial entrepreneurs lack most. Entrepreneurs build things and solve problems for people, but according to this study they do this in hopes of a return on investment... which people with high empathy do not generally expect.*

b) *Entrepreneurial-minded people are not proficient in* **managing themselves** *and their time. Often they need assistance managing everyday tasks and should hire or delegate them to someone who has mastered this skill.*

c) *This leads to another skill that entrepreneurs lack:* **planning and organizing**. *Hiring someone to keep their calendar, organize meetings and events, keep the office de-cluttered, and help keep them on schedule can put them at an advantage.*

d) *Entrepreneurs also do not excel above the control group when it comes to* **analytical problem solving**. *Entrepreneurs have the vision, but need to employ people to create an executable strategy and carry it through.*

THE FOUR KEY SKILLS SUCCESSFUL ENTREPRENEURS HAVE (Not to miss any trait!)

Entrepreneurs wanting to be successful are urged to acquire these skills. After all, it does not require any talent or cost to develop these skills; all that is required is an investment of time and effort.

LISTENING: The success of your business depends on how you solve your customer's problems. Attentive listening is critical to understand the challenges to help provide real solutions.

PRIORITIZATION: All tasks are not created equal. You need to prioritize what is important at a given point of time to your strategic goals.

RESPONSIVENESS: It costs you nothing to be more responsive ; instantly make your customers happier.

OPENNESS: Keep an open mind.

A TENTATIVE CONCLUSION ON ENTREPRENEURIAL TRAITS

Despite the irresistible temptation to discover a bunch of neat or easily definable attributes of successful entrepreneurs, all that we can surmise with some certainty are:

a) All of us are born with a range of qualities; what one does with them is mostly a function of the environment in which one lives and learns.

b) Every entrepreneur has a set of traits, skills and strengths, either born with or acquired or both. Not that all successful entrepreneurs have all the traits identified.

c) The trick is not taking any trait too far. After all, risk-taking can lead to being reckless. Attention to

d) detail can become obsessive and, therefore, counter-productive or calm can become an unemotional response or self-confidence becoming hubris. Level-headedness or balance holds the key.

Notwithstanding the several reservations stated above, the undying fascination with the concept of the 'entrepreneurial person' shall remain for long.

In the final analysis, what matters most is motivation - whether or not one is unreservedly enthusiastic about being an entrepreneur and is willing to relentlessly pursue such goals as are set, no matter how tough the challenges are.

Only a few in every society take the road less travelled to become an entrepreneur.

3.7 WHY IS AN ENTREPRENEUR, AN ENTREPRENEUR?

"To leave behind a piece of you" - The Economist

How an entrepreneur takes the decision to start a new venture has been characterized as a scientifically unfathomable mystery, some kind of an intuitive judgment.

Two Dutch economists, Dr. Bulat Sanditov and Dr. Bart Verspagen, have broadly classified the factors influencing individual decisions to pursue entrepreneurship as a career option (as opposed to safe, salaried employment) into two sets of factors:

1. **Individual factors**: Demographic (gender, age, marital status, family background), wealth, income, current working status, individual human capital (education, professional experience and expertise), personal/psychological traits (risk attitude, over-optimism, preference for independence)

2. **Social factors**: Social capital and social norms, macro-economic conditions (per capita income, financial system, availability of credit, pro-enterprise policies etc.)

The report of the National Knowledge Commission, India proposes that in most cases entrepreneurs are driven by their own inner drive:

1. Wanting to be independent - *'freedom to do one's own thing'*.
2. The compelling need to take on the challenges offered by an entrepreneurial career.
3. Accomplishing the long-cherished dream of becoming an entrepreneur. Market opportunities offered by a supporting overall environment encourage the initial decision of an individual to become an entrepreneur.
4. The response of a sample of existing entrepreneurs to the question what had motivated them to become entrepreneurs has been as follows:
    a) Independence: 21%
    b) Family background: 21%
    c) Market opportunity: 19%
    d) Idea-driven: 18%

e) Challenge: 11%
f) Dream/desire: 10%

Some distinct inspirations

a) Some take the trip out of necessity
b) Some out of a sense of adventure
c) Some simply evolve into business
d) Some out of a sense of determination
e) Wanting to take on an activity where discipline, dedication and intelligent hard work give results.
f) Seizing a great idea, an opportunity of high potential.
g) For the joy and satisfaction that comes from creation and problem solving. Seeking self-esteem: Strong feeling of accomplishment and contentment when one achieves what one sets out to.
h) Being able to exercise creativity in a way that is not possible in the traditional workspace, devoting oneself to something one likes, something that would be impossible if one were not an entrepreneur.
i) Self-expression: Building businesses to express themselves or their abilities; expression of skills, talents, passions and creativity. Proving oneself to others or proving something to oneself.
j) Sustaining family legacy/family opportunity; leaving a personal legacy behind serves as a motivation.
k) Wanting to achieve financial security to have the surplus to spend on activities/causes close to one's heart, have a satisfying life style.
l) Achieving success for its own sake; having the ambition to be as successful as one can be
m) A desire to recover assets lost by the family.
n) Driven by intrinsic motivation to work on something because it is interesting, involving, exciting, satisfying or personally challenging.
o) Money & Fame: Along with business success comes fame, prestige and limelight.

p) A survey of nearly 550 founders of companies by Global Engineering and Entrepreneurship, Duke University, USA, found that the important motivations for becoming entrepreneurs are building wealth, owning a company, start-up culture and capitalizing on a business idea.

Then again, an extensive survey of entrepreneurs by Ernst & Young revealed that "making a difference" was the most common response when asked what motivated them professionally; "making money" was the least common.

"Build wealth as a byproduct of your business success. If wealth is your only objective in business, you will probably fail." - J. Paul Getty, a highly successful American industrialist.

q) No degrees or pieces of paper stand in one's way; even learning disabilities cannot stop one wanting to be an entrepreneur.

r) Controlling one's own destiny is considered the greatest motivator for choosing the path of self-employment. Wanting to be one's own boss; be independent having the control and freedom to make one's own decisions/one's own rules; have the freedom to reconcile one's professional life with one's personal life. **The irony indeed is that whomsoever an entrepreneur does business with becomes his boss. In fact, the entrepreneur is accountable to multiple bosses - also known as his customers.**

Philosophically, it could be argued that entrepreneurship is not about the entrepreneur or about his getting rich or about his proving something to the world or about his struggling to overcome odds. It is about the entrepreneur helping other people achieve their goals, satisfying customers by helping them save money or solve problems or feel good.

The contrarian view to the above is that while serving others is the cardinal goal, ignoring the real reasons you are doing it can be counter-productive. After all, disregarding your own self-interests while helping others can only last so long.

3.8 WHAT DOES AN ENTREPRENEUR DO?

"A business is not just an activity. Golf is an activity. A business must create something that someone, somewhere, somehow will pay to have. Business is about creating value. The value must manifest in terms of products and

services generating revenues and profits as well as benefits to consumers and stakeholders." - Rebel Holiday, ezineArticles.com

Entrepreneurs build new businesses - create something out of nothing - turn around old ones. They struggle day and night, sometimes succeed but often fail. Nonetheless, they are resilient and they keep on coming.

Vadim Kotelnikov, founder of Ten3 Business e-Coach, identified the following 3 sets of tasks, which a successful entrepreneur does:

1. **Visioning and setting the example**: Creates an inspiring vision and shared values; leads change; leads by example; demonstrates confidence.
2. **Empowering and energizing**: Inspires and energizes people; empowers people; communicates openly; listens, supports and helps.
3. **Leading teams**: Involves everyone, uses team approach; coaches, brings out the best in your people; encourages group discussions; monitors programmes, but avoids micromanaging.

More specifically, an entrepreneur:

1. Identifies the present and potential customers (of the products planned to be marketed by the enterprise) and assesses what they want.
2. Identifies and evaluates other enterprises that market similar products and, therefore, represent the competition.
3. Analyses the data on the consumer and competition to zero in on a segment/niche of the market offering the best potential to benefit from.
4. Develops a Business Plan depicting step-by-step action plan to exploit the business opportunities the identified niche offers.
5. Creates an appropriate organization and mobilizes the resources - finance, people, physical facilities, technology etc. - to convert the opportunity into a marketable product.

Such entrepreneurial efforts are driven by the expectation that the business will earn more than the time, energy and money an entrepreneur has invested. In the process, he takes on the risks of losing the investments, the time and the reputation.

Most successful entrepreneurs have trouble articulating how they did what they did. May be they are unconsciously competent. They just do it but cannot explain how. That very few entrepreneurs spawn successful entrepreneurs around them is cited as the evidence.

3.9 SOME MYTHS ABOUT ENTREPRENEURS

1. **Entrepreneurs are born, not made** - Refer to the discussion at 3.4.

2. A widely accepted attribute of an entrepreneur is **tolerance for risk**. In fact, some may even take wild risks; the resultant uncertainties can be so big, such risk-taking sometimes may lead to a ruinous end. Fundamentally, entrepreneurs are not risk-seekers; they are not afraid of the unknown either. They essentially take calculated risks where the odds are *"heads I win, tails I don't lose much"*. They are consummate practitioners of the art of shifting the odds in their favor. The smarter of them manage to spread the risk around to others - employees, suppliers, customers etc.

   Michel Villette and Catherine Vuillermot, the French scholars, who wrote *From Predators to Icons*, believe that the truly successful businessman is anything but a risk-taker. He is a predator and predators seek to incur the least risk possible while hunting.

   Malcolm Gladwell, the celebrated author, recently attempted an explanation of this myth about entrepreneurial traits and stated, *"The entrepreneur takes risks but doesn't see himself as a risk-taker, because he operates under the useful delusion that what he is attempting is not risky. Then, (half way through) people discover the truth - and, because it is too late to turn back, they are forced to finish the job."*

3. **Most successful entrepreneurs start with highly innovative products:** Yes, some do; some products can be radical, disruptive and game-changing breakthroughs. Most, however, offer a better 'Mousetrap.' In fact, many offer 'Mousetraps' of the same functionality at a lower price or via more convenient distribution networks to win customers. Some could even offer the service (of trapping mice) rather than the device!

   Many successful entrepreneurs are found to concentrate on processes rather than products, particularly in the Services Sector.

4. **To succeed, you have got to be smart**: Of course, successful entrepreneurs have been smart in the way they define their role in taking on the world; not necessarily in the way society generally defines smartness. Significant proportion of millionaire entrepreneurs worldwide did not have the time or motivation to complete a graduation programme.

   Fortune 500 CEOs who dropped out of high school or university and became full-time entrepreneurs and self-made billionaires include Bill Gates, Larry Page (Google), Michael Dell (Dell), David Geffen (Geffen Records), Steve Jobs, Richard Branson, Ralph Lauren (Luxury clothing business), Jerry Yang (Yahoo) and Mark Zuckerberg (Facebook). Henry Ford was trained only as a machinist.

   In fact, being one of the smartest guys on the planet is no qualification to become a successful entrepreneur. Einstein's father, a serial entrepreneur but not particularly a successful one, wanted his son to follow his footsteps. According to a version, Einstein did, in fact, try to manage his father's business for a brief while. The outcome was not precisely something Einstein Sr. or Einstein Jr. wanted to be reminded of!

   Successful entrepreneurs are not necessarily Type A - an overachieving, hyper organized workaholic or an extrovert. Very often, it could be Type C students who become entrepreneurs.

   That said, today's new breed of entrepreneurs in the knowledge industry like Bill Gates, Pierre Omidyar (founder of eBay), Larry Page and Sergey Brin, Steve Jobs, Evan Williams (co-founder of Twitter) and Mark Zuckerberg are exceptionally smart people who relentlessly pursued their vision to create businesses never before imagined.

5. That **entrepreneurship is the fountain of youth:** Willingness to take risk declines with age. A few of the most flamboyantly successful entrepreneurs of our times happen to be young, almost all of them in the IT space. Especially for Internet firms, Startup costs tend to be low and prior business experience is not a pre-condition for success. But, for most other businesses experience does count.

   The studies done by Kauffman Foundation and Vivek Wadhwa demonstrate that the average age of successful Startup founders in such industries as biotech, business software and other high-growth segments was 40. Many successful entrepreneurs - Harland Sanders of Kentucky Fried Chicken; Gary Burrell of Garmin, a GPS giant; Herb Kelleher of South West Airlines; and Dhirubhai Ambani of Reliance Group, India - were relatively older.

6. **You need lots of money**: Some of the largest US companies were launched out of a garage or college dormitory or elsewhere on slender financial stamina: Disney, Harley Davidson, Yankee Candle Company, Maglite, Microsoft, Dell Computers, Oracle, Amazon, Apple, Google, Hewlett-Packard, Nike, Mattel and Facebook, all had small beginnings.

    Indian IT giant Infosys was started with a capital of just $250 (Valuation of the company as in Feb 2015 was over $40 billion). Kiran Mazumdar-Shaw started BioCon, the Bangalore-based emerging global pharmaceutical enterprise, in a garage on an initial capital of Rs. 10,000 (The company was valued at Rs. 87 billion as in Mar 2015); Liu Chuanzhi built Lenovo (which acquired IBM's PC unit in 2005) as a Startup in 1984 in a dusty, two-room Beijing guardhouse.

7. **A detailed Business Plan is critical**: The evidence indicating a strong relationship between Business Plan and success may not be compelling, especially in the case of new-age enterprises. The most important pre-requisite is responding creatively to the needs of customers after learning what they are looking for. A good team and smart execution are other success factors.

    The process of conceptualizing, planning, executing and managing businesses need not necessarily be based on carefully researched, rigorously analyzed and comprehensively thought-through grand plans in all contexts.

    An entrepreneur interviewed by Amar Bhide said, *"... The process of starting a new business is like jumping from rock to rock up a stream rather than constructing the Golden Gate Bridge from a detailed blue print."*

    In most cases, successful business founders jumped into the fray and just started doing without having to have a detailed business plan.

    There is also the argument that a Business Plan is an operating document to help address the "knowns". But most Startups tend to face a series of unknowns - unknown customer segments, unknown customer needs, unknown product features etc.

Steve Jobs (Apple Inc.) famously said, "**We do no market research. We just want to make great products.**" But then, Jobs was a genius. Urging others to do diligent research and careful planning before taking on any entrepreneurial initiative is smart advice.

8. Most successful entrepreneurs have a **strong track record and years of experience in their industries:** Many successful entrepreneurs had no experience at the beginning. They did indeed possess a set of traits the entrepreneurs are typically endowed with, a set of unique talents, which help them learn fast and get around such challenges as they face.

9. That entrepreneurs are "**orphans and outcasts**" engaged in a lonely pursuit of their goals amidst a hostile environment. Entrepreneurship, like all businesses, is a social activity and requires business partners and social networks for success.

10. That entrepreneurship is driven **mainly by Venture Capital**. But Venture Capitalists fund only a small fraction of Startups (Less than 1% of new businesses started each year in the US receive venture funding). Most of such ventures are funded by the promoters' savings or personal debt or from the "three Fs" - Friends, Family and Fools!

3.10 TEN DEADLY MISTAKES ENTREPRENEURS COMMIT

1. **Discovering a solution without defining a problem**
    - Not defining the target customer group or assessing their precise requirements or designing the right product to meet customer requirements.
2. **Over-estimating market potential and under-estimating market competition**
3. **Deficient marketing**
    - Price not low enough to attract customers to buy or high enough to earn a profit
    - Not choosing the appropriate distribution network
    - Weak advertising and sales promotion

4. **Poor financial management**
   - Failure to anticipate a financial crisis thereby failing to take timely actions
5. **Founding team falling apart too soon**
6. **Weak management processes**
   - Poor planning/lack of contingency plans
   - Poor task prioritization
   - Inefficient delegation or failure to delegate to the right people
   - Setting no goals or setting unrealistic goals
7. **Choice of inappropriate technology or scale of operation**
8. **Bad location of the enterprise.**
9. **Failing by scaling – uncontrolled growth**
10. **Not doing the right thing or not doing things right**

The latest discovery

Alexa Clay and Kyra Maya Phillips discover a group of people who are just as innovative, entrepreneurial and visionary as the Jobs' or Edisons' or Fords' of the world. They display remarkable ingenuity, pioneering original methods and practices that we can learn from and apply in conventional contexts. They are the pirates, bootleggers, hustlers, counterfeiters and computer hackers living in the black, grey and informal economies.

The duo's book, *"The Misfit Economy: Lessons in Creativity from Pirates, Hackers, Gangsters and Other Informal Entrepreneurs"* (Published in June 2015 by Simon & Schuster), argues that misfits can make the best innovators because frustration with the status quo spurs their desire to change it. More than money, the real motivators are personality quirks: Idealism, ambition, curiosity and stubbornness. They are driven by:

a) Restless energy that creates something from nothing through tenacity and resourcefulness.

b) The desire "to force destiny, to create serendipity."

4
Unraveling The Mystique Of Entrepreneurship

Understanding why small businesses fail or succeed is fundamental to the designing of appropriate strategies for ensuring sustainable and inclusive socio-economic development of every country.

4.1 DEFINING ENTREPRENEURSHIP

"Entrepreneurship refers to an individual's ability to turn ideas into action. It includes creativity, innovation and taking calculated risks as well as the ability to plan and manage projects in order to achieve objectives... Entrepreneurship is the mindset and process to create and develop economic activity by building risk-taking creativity and/or innovation with sound management, within a new or an existing organization." - European Commission, 2008.

"The art of identifying viable business opportunities and mobilizing the resources to convert the opportunity into a successful enterprise through creativity, innovation, risk-taking and progressive imagination", ILO Youth Entrepreneurship Manual, 2009.

Joseph Schumpeter described entrepreneurship as the creation of new resource combinations through the art of innovation. It transforms underutilized resources into new uses, enables the creation of new industries and unleashes *"gales of creative destruction"*

Entrepreneurship is an amalgam of the art and science of finding creative solutions to the problems which consumers face, solutions which yield a minimum acceptable and sustainable profit to the entrepreneur for his pains. It has been described as the process through which 'private obsession' fulfills 'public need'.

Then there is the pithy definition: *"Entrepreneurship, first and foremost, is a mindset, the art of finding profitable solutions to problems... before somebody else does."*

Business entrepreneurship starts with an entrepreneur who has a novel idea, an innovative product, a creative approach to solving a perceived problem, a new business model (mode of revenue generation) or a previously untried approach to the delivery of the product or service.

Entrepreneurship involves the creation of something new, creation of a new venture as a new economic activity. The new economic activity could be:

a) The conversion of a new idea into a successful innovation and new product, new to the market.

b) Innovation producing a product new to the firm but not new to the market; a new economic activity of existing firms as a diversification.

Entrepreneurship is about inventing the future. Because it:

1. Creates new products, new processes to meet the needs of customers.

2. Identifies and exploits new markets in the sense that some of the customers may not have been in the market for the new product category in the past. True innovation creates something never existed before; it helps consumers to do something they could not do before. Even creating a product at lower costs can create a new customer base. IT industry, for instance, has generated several new products/services and corresponding customer groups.

3. Generates new jobs that never existed before.

Entrepreneurship is not for the faint-hearted. It is a journey into the unknown and the entrepreneur needs to be comfortable with taking on ambiguity, uncertainty and multiple challenges. It is a difficult, taxing and essentially unforgiving career choice, which, if got right (through own efforts or sheer luck), can be highly rewarding in financial terms as well as in terms of the indescribable sense of accomplishment.

Other characteristics of entrepreneurship include:

a) Entrepreneurship and Startups are not one and the same. Not all businesses or Startups are necessarily entrepreneurial (in the strict sense of the term which purists propound); besides business entrepreneurship, there is social entrepreneurship.

b) Entrepreneurial activities are not uniquely the preserve of small firms; large companies can also be entrepreneurial, translating a new idea into a product.

c) All entrepreneurial businesses do not succeed. However, even failed businesses can still be entrepreneurial and their promoters can be entrepreneurs.

Is entrepreneurship an art or a science? Is it learned or instinctive? Could its existence be formulated and, thereby, predicted? Nobody knows for sure.

A faculty member of Harvard Business School described the field of entrepreneurship as an intellectual onion. *"You peel it back layer by layer and when you get to the core, there is nothing there, but you are crying!"*

ARE ALL BUSINESSES FUNDAMENTALLY THE SAME? YES. AND NO.

Regardless of whether the business is small or large, new or old, successful or failing, they all are based on the same basic building blocks: People, material, equipment, facilities, money and knowledge. These elements are combined to create a product to delight a set of customers who are willing to pay the asking price to what you offer.

But then, businesses, even in the same product category, are fundamentally different: Different people with different competencies, motivations, cultures and expectations, operating in different environments and could well be catering to different sets of customers.

Despite endless attempts at discovering general principles, more often than not, we realize that **each successful or not-so-successful entrepreneur has a 'unique recipe' for what he does and how he does it**.

4.2 DEFINING STARTUPS

The term Startup has been bandied about with increasing frequency over the past few years. Let us try to define the concept from different perspectives to get a sense of it.

a) A Startup is a small business that has just been started.

b) A newly established business entity attempting to solve a problem when the solution is not obvious and success is not guaranteed.

c) Startup means "the act or an instance of setting in operation or motion or a fledgling business enterprise" - Merriam and Webster.

d) "A business or undertaking that has recently begun operation" - The American Heritage Dictionary.

e) A Startup is a temporary organization attempting to search for a repeatable and scalable business model. It wants to grow to being a large business; if it fails, then move on to another opportunity.

f) A company that is in the first stage of its operation.

g) Early stage in the lifecycle of an enterprise when the entrepreneur moves from the idea stage to securing finance, putting in place the basic structure of the business and initiating operations or trading.

The general notion is that Startups are technology-driven or tech companies. Startups often adapt technology to solve problems. But a Startup, by definition, need not be tech-oriented.

Scalability or ability to grow fast is the key attribute of a Startup. This feature differentiates it from small businesses. By this definition, a restaurant in one town is not a Startup nor is a franchise a Startup.

Government of India's definition of Startup (Startup-India Action Plan, January 2016)

Startup means an entity, incorporated or registered (Private Limited Company or a Registered Partnership Firm) in India not prior to five years, with annual turnover not exceeding Rs. 250 million in any preceding financial year, working towards innovation, development, deployment or commercialization of new products, processes or services driven by technology or intellectual property (Provided that such an entity is not formed by splitting up or reconstruction of an already existing business).

A business is covered under the definition if it aims to develop and commercialize a new product or service or process; or a significantly improved existing product or service or process that will create or add value for customers or workflow.

The above definition provides an all-embracing concept which would mean that any new unit which generates employment by meeting an unmet demand of society or meet a met demand more effectively - better quality or lower cost product/service.

4.3 MODELS OF ENTREPRENEURSHIP

A study done by Accenture, the international consulting group, describes 3 broad models of entrepreneurship: The Free Market Model, the Guided Individualism Model and the Social Democratic Model.

1. *The Free Market Model: The US is the prime example characterized by minimal government intervention in the economy, an approach considered to be the best way to maintain incentives for entrepreneurial behaviour. Deregulation helps clear barriers that get in the way of entrepreneurship.*

2. *The Guided Individualism Model: This model emphasizes greater involvement of government, with the aid of public policies, to influence the broad sweep and direction of entrepreneurial energies. It supports individual enterprise and has been successful in Taiwan and Singapore.*

3. *The Social Democratic Model: Countries such as Germany, the Netherlands and Sweden are wedded to this model. Government plays an important role in creating the right environment for entrepreneurial growth with social protection.*

4.4 DIFFERENT STAGES OF ENTREPRENEURIAL LIFECYCLE

Saras D. Saraswathy, faculty of Darden School of Business, posits the following questions:

1. How did someone make the decision to leave a well-paying, secure job to strike out on his own?
2. What were the antecedents, triggers and processes that brought him to that decision?
3. What other options, if any, did he consider at the point of that decision and what criteria did he use to choose among them?
4. What is the role of contingency as opposed to luck, in all of this?

A nascent entrepreneur represents the beginning of entrepreneurship. Nascent entrepreneurs are those who are actively planning to set up a new business that they will personally own and manage. The transition from a pre-nascent or prospective entrepreneur to new business ownership can be thought of as a process comprising 7 phases:

1. Nurturing an intention to start a business.
2. Opportunity identification: Researching and understanding the different aspects of the opportunity, the concept itself and trying to figure out how to decide whether it is attractive or not with the aid of a Business Plan and zeroes in on a narrowly defined opportunity.
3. Mobilizing the resources (funds, physical facilities, people, technology etc.) and creating an organization to manage the business.
4. Market entry: When first sales are made
5. Full launch and growth
6. Maturity and expansion: Professional management practices drive the company; can be a market leader or close to being a leader or merely one of the players.
7. Liquidity event: Harvesting stage to capture the value created; typical exits (in part or full) are Initial Public Offering or being acquired by mostly a larger firm.

4.5 IS ENTREPRENEURSHIP LEARNABLE AND, THEREFORE, TEACHABLE?

A takeoff from the born versus made conundrum relating to entrepreneur, entrepreneurship education is a subject of intense debates without a consensus in sight; the divide between the nay-sayers and the aye-sayers is just about as wide.

THE 'ART' AND 'SCIENCE' OF ENTREPRENEURSHIP EDUCATION & TRAINING

Over the past more than a decade, there has been an explosion of entrepreneurship education and training (EET) programmes across the world, based on the hypothesis that such programmes promote the mindsets, attitudes and skills to identify business opportunities and exploit them. Today, EET is recognized as an established field of study representing both formal academic education and stand-alone training programmes.

EET has two broad components - the Art and the Science:

1. The Art represents such psychological traits of the entrepreneur as creativity, innovative thinking, intuition, self-confidence, leadership, a positive attitude towards risk, motivation, personal need for achievement and a passion to win, tenacity, optimism and emotional intelligence.
2. The Science of EET encompasses overall awareness and perception of entrepreneurship, general business knowledge and skills needed for launching and managing new businesses including marketing, mobilization of funds, people management, financial literacy and soft skills.

EET can provide individuals the cognitive ability to leverage their respective skills and abilities to exploit potential entrepreneurial opportunities.

EET targets a wide range of individuals and has a variety of programme objectives. For Secondary School students, the programme will be to enhance their socio-emotional skills. For Under Graduates and Graduates enrolled in formal degree granting programmes, EET would cover exploring business opportunities and the development of Business Plans to translate the ideas into enterprises.

The training interventions are essentially designed for the benefit of potential and practicing entrepreneurs who are not part of formal degree granting programmes. The potential entrepreneurs range from, at one end, unemployed, inactive individuals or necessity-driven potential entrepreneurs (who take to entrepreneurship or self-employment to escape from being unemployed) to highly skilled, innovation-led potential entrepreneurs, at the other end. Practicing entrepreneurs are exposed to whole range of capacity-building training modules, which enhance their entrepreneurial and managerial capabilities.

Growthink.com, a US-based business planning, strategy consulting, and investment banking services, looked at the educational qualifications of the top hundred US entrepreneurs of today to answer the question whether level of education impacts entrepreneurial activities. While 93% attended college, only 72% of them graduated; 15% of entrepreneurs earned their MBAs. These ratios tend to be much higher than those relating to general public.

YOU CAN'T TEACH PASSION!

The unbridled enthusiasm for entrepreneurship education cannot mask a somewhat awkward aspect of entrepreneurship education - it is some kind of a black box embedded within which are indeterminable features. There is the Teachability Dilemma arising from the considerable conceptual confusion regarding what entrepreneurship education is and what it aims to accomplish.

One can get lost when one explores answers to the questions of whom to teach what and how. Because it is difficult to design the content, the methodology and the duration of such programmes to match the needs of the target groups.

Despite claims to the contrary, teaching the Art of entrepreneurship is exceedingly difficult. Because, the traits identified early on (in this book) are so tough to observe, measure, diffuse and nurture. Many believe that some of the important entrepreneurial traits are part of the genetic make-up of a person.

"Entrepreneurship is about having guts - something professors cannot teach... The steps you have to take, the risks you have to take... I don't think in a million years you can teach it in a classroom." - Paul Fleming, founder of a highly successful restaurant chain.

Ultimately, building a successful enterprise is about passion. *"The passion for your business is not something you can learn in a classroom"* - Doris Christopher, the founder of The Pampered Chef, a global venture.

"Can you mass-produce the serendipity that forms the core of so many breakthrough ventures?... Trying to mass-produce Startups is like trying to manufacture musicians or painters." - TIME, March 25, 2013

Prof. Murray Hunter, a serial entrepreneur, academic and essayist, makes a powerful statement that teaching entrepreneurship is a myth. Many courses currently being offered are teaching about entrepreneurship rather than teaching entrepreneurship.

Another skeptic is Prof. Scott Shane, Professor of Entrepreneurial Studies at the Case Western Reserve University. He is not particularly enthused about the process of teaching/learning entrepreneurship or its merits. His arguments are:

a) Entrepreneurial talent cannot be quickly built by giving people a short course in writing a business plan or using Quick Books.

b) Despite a wide range of government programmes for increasing the stock of entrepreneurs, there has always been only a limited supply of people capable of creating and running successful businesses.

Obviously, every innovation is new and unique and no formal education system can dictate concrete terms to be innovative or to be entrepreneurial.

Even the best of entrepreneurship education cannot accelerate the rate of Startup promotion; a whole range of other enablers has to be in place.

> **Case Study: Hamara Dhandha of NITIE, Mumbai**
>
> National Institute of Industrial Engineering (Managed by HRD Ministry, Government of India) is one of the top Engineering and Business Schools in the country with excellent placement record over the years. Hamara Dhandha has been an initiative of NITIE since 2007 to encourage students to promote enterprises, targeting those who had taken entrepreneurship development elective. Initially, **only 1% went ahead with their ventures after leaving the Institute, others opted for traditional placement channels.**

LEARNING AND TEACHING ENTREPRENEURSHIP

"Entrepreneurship is neither a science nor an art. It is a practice"... "Most of what you hear about entrepreneurship is all wrong. It's not magic; it's not mysterious; and it has nothing to do with genes. It is a discipline and, like any discipline, it can be learned." - Peter F. Drucker, Management Guru

"... Entrepreneurship was not a black art, but rather comprised of a set of skills that could be learnt and taught." - Kauffman Foundation

Entrepreneurialism is identified as one of the major forces shaping the 21st century business education environment.

"Entrepreneurship and education are two extraordinary opportunities that need to be leveraged and interconnected if we are to develop the human capital required for building the societies of the future" - Klaus Schwab, Founder and Executive Chairman, World Economic Forum.

"We believe entrepreneurial skills, attitudes and behaviours can be learned." - World Economic Forum, Nov 9, 2009.

Successful entrepreneurs demonstrate a certain behavioural pattern: They evaluate carefully opportunities and plan every step of the way before taking on a venture, assemble the right resources and are good at confronting adversities and managing growth. Entrepreneurship education shall help create attitudes, skills and behaviours in the mindsets of young people, getting students positively consider entrepreneurship as an attractive career, a real alternative to paid employment or unemployment.

Bringing entrepreneurship and market into the classroom can bring about changing attitudes and motives leading to concrete actions only if the process of learning is experiential and problem-based. The methodology should include case studies, interaction with successful entrepreneurs, internship, business visits and business plan preparation. In other words, the teaching should focus on experiencing entrepreneurship rather than simply teaching knowledge on business creation.

Many of the underlying requirements for entrepreneurship, such as the ability to analyze opportunities, assemble resources and structure an economic organization can be taught, despite the notion that it is a way of thinking.

Business schools teach the value of frameworks, strategic and quantitative tools to appraise the opportunities. They also teach collaborative and fact-based approach to decision-making.

World Economic Forum presents the following agenda for educating the entrepreneurs:

1. What

Enhancing entrepreneurial behaviours and mindsets; Building self-confidence, self-efficacy and leadership;

Creativity, innovation and ability to think out-of-the-box to solve problems; Basic business and financial skills: 'business literacy'; Managing complexity and unpredictability; How to build, finance and grow ventures; Opportunity identification; Building relationships, networks, social capital; Developing negotiation skills.

2. How

Classroom/Informal learning/Mentoring/ Networking/Simulations/ Internship/Case Studies/

Metaphors /Games; External use of visually digital tools and multi-media; Learning by doing/hands-on; Experimental learning/labs (trial & error); Projects, internships with start-ups; Mentoring and coaching; Interaction with entrepreneurs.

3. Who

Students, Teachers, Professors, Entrepreneurs, Mentors, Coaches and Advisors

4. Where

Formal school system; Informal system; Community centers; NGOs; Government agencies; Banks; Life- long learning.

5. Focus

Joy of business, wealth creation, ownership, meeting the needs of people; Market opportunity recognition and research; Empathy ("walk in your customers' shoes"); Comparative advantage; Laws of supply and demand; Return on Investment (RoI) and Break-even calculations.

World Economic Forum at its meeting in India on the theme of **Redesigning India's Entrepreneurial Ecosystem: India**

Economic Summit (Nov 9, 2009) made the following suggestions for entrepreneurship learning:

a) Education is the key to innovation and high growth entrepreneurship. "Education can ignite entrepreneurship".

b) Entrepreneurship education should not be regarded as an option only for those who fail or do not perform well in school. It should be embedded, if not compulsory, across all levels of education and in all types of colleges, including elite institutions.

c) The links between the business sector and academia must be strengthened.

d) Need for families to overcome their fear of failure and avoid passing it to their children, which in turn prevents them from trying new ventures and projects, even at primary and secondary school levels.

e) Alignment of all stakeholders of the ecosystem (parents, teachers, business community, civil society, government) into the advancement of innovative entrepreneurship in India.

f) More engagement from the business sector and government leaders to serve as mentors/role models for young/potential entrepreneurs.

g) Need to strengthen the links between business and higher education institutions to bring more innovation into firms.

h) Need for innovative approaches at school that develop children's creativity at an early age and nurture it throughout the education process.

i) Promoting more programmes addressing financial literacy, basic numeracy and management skills.

UNCTAD Guidelines to enhance Entrepreneurship Education & Skills Development

1. Embed entrepreneurship in formal and informal education

a) Mainstream the development of entrepreneurship awareness and entrepreneurial behaviours starting from primary school level (e.g. risk taking, teamwork behaviours, etc.).

b) Promote entrepreneurship through electives, extracurricular activities, career awareness seminars and visits to businesses at secondary school level.
c) Support entrepreneurship courses, programmes and chairs at higher education institutions and universities.
d) Promote vocational training and apprenticeship programmes.
e) Promote and link up with entrepreneurship training centers.

2. **Develop effective entrepreneurship curricula**
   a) Prepare basic entrepreneurial skills education material.
   b) Encourage tailored local material, case studies and role models.
   c) Foster interactive and on-line tools.
   d) Promote experiential and learning-by-doing methodologies.

3. **Train teachers**
   a) Ensure teachers engage with the private sector and with entrepreneurs and support initiatives that bring entrepreneurs to educational establishments.
   b) Encourage entrepreneurship training for teachers.
   c) Promote entrepreneurship educators' networks.

4. **Partner with the private sector**
   a) Encourage private sector sponsorship for entrepreneurship training and skill development.
   b) Link up business with entrepreneurship education networks.
   c) Develop mentoring programmes.

US ENTREPRENEURIAL EDUCATION SCENE

In the US, there is a staggering range of entrepreneurship education from K-12 programmes for promoting an understanding of entrepreneurship among students to PhD programmes.

Entrepreneurship education has become the hottest topic at US Business/Engineering Schools. There were about 2200 courses, 1600 schools, close to 300 Endowment positions in over 100 established centers, as relating to 2010 or thereabout.

The curriculum generally covers core business courses like Accounting, Economics, Finance and Marketing. Required entrepreneurship courses include creativity and innovation, entrepreneurship, new venture business planning, organizational design alternatives, product development and management, business plans, venture finance, social entrepreneurship, business ethics and laws for entrepreneurs.

Select schools in the US are pioneering an educational innovation by offering certificate programmes in what they call "Minimum Viable Product" or MBA Lite:

a) Falling job opportunities and prevailing high unemployment rates are encouraging students to embrace entrepreneurship. More undergraduate business students than ever before are launching Startups right after graduation. In fact, some promote enterprises while still at school. This process is facilitated by technology, especially the Internet and the ever-expanding social media. Educational institutions are vigorously and creatively responding to this need.

b) Currently over 300 post-secondary institutions offer entrepreneurship and small-business certificate programmes as compared to 72 institutions 15 years earlier.

c) Drawing upon the popular approach to software development, institutions are offering a Minimum Viable Product which is defined by Eric Ries as *"the product which has those core features (and no more) that allows you to ship a product that resonates with early adopters, some of whom will pay you money and give you feedback"*. The recently launched Venture College offers a 2 semester programme that introduces students to the basics of entrepreneurship with mentoring support by experienced professionals, entrepreneurs and Venture Capitalists.

d) MBA Lite programmes are short-term courses at a fraction of the costs of a typical MBA. Such courses help the people to get their businesses off the ground. The topics covered include marketing, financial management, tax and legal issues, business plans, pricing, fund-raising and customer service. The course will also arrange meeting with mentors and potential investors.

A TENTATIVE CONCLUSION

"If Thomas Edison had gone to a Business School, we would all be reading by large candles!" - Mark McCormack, *What they don't teach you at Harvard*

Is there a learnable and teachable core to entrepreneurship? Yes and No. Can teachers make people entrepreneurs? No. Only a certain kind of people might be drawn to entrepreneurship - a career that is characterized by unimaginable uncertainties, ambiguities and complexities.

Entrepreneurship is often thought of as a way of thinking and a business education/training may not transform people into entrepreneurs. However, insights into accounting and financial management, market research, writing business plans, exploring and evaluating opportunities etc. can be had through education.

Whether an entrepreneur is "born" or "made", professional training can upgrade the skills to improve the decision-making process thereby raising the chances of success of an enterprise.

Professional experiences - Startup experience, general management experience and industry-specific experience - arguably are more helpful than any kind of academic programmes. Because, they provide the tacit knowledge to address real-life issues which entrepreneurs face when promoting and managing new enterprises.

The impact analysis of EE programmes around the world shows mixed, modest results when it comes to enterprise creation, improved business outcomes and employment generation by those entrepreneurs who participated in such programmes.

In India, entrepreneurship programmes of varying duration and quality have vigorously been pursued in all the States for several years. The effectiveness of such programmes - the number of participants of such programmes promoting successful enterprises - is uncertain. The general impression is that the hit rate is woefully low.

4.6 INNOVATION AND ENTREPRENEURSHIP

Especially in developed countries, innovation (enhancing productivity across all sectors) is being treated as the most important factor of production fostering economic growth. Pioneering entrepreneurial

Startups are the source of continued societal dynamism and prosperity because the older, easier sources of growth are drying up.

Invention, innovation and entrepreneurship are fuzzy, overlapping concepts that have been given multiple meanings.

1. Inventor is a thinker, a problem solver who achieves a technical breakthrough thereby creating a new possibility or a new product idea.
2. Innovator develops that possibility to usefulness or marketability. Innovator uses the new knowledge to create a new product, which solves a customer problem more effectively than existing products. (In some cases, the consumer had not even thought he had a problem till the innovative firm points it up!)
3. Invention or innovation is worthless unless it creates a customer. Entrepreneur discovers customers. Entrepreneur is a doer driven to act, to build. In many cases, innovators take on the role of entrepreneurs.

Creation of value distinguishes innovation from its typical predecessors: Invention and creativity. Innovation is *"New ideas - plus action or implementation - which result in an improvement, a gain or a profit"* - 3M, the American multinational conglomerate. 'Value' is defined in a broad way to include higher value added to the firm and benefits to customers including other firms.

Stages of innovation

Research & Development **LEADS TO** Inventions/Blueprints **LEADS TO** Prototypes/Beta version **LEADS TO** IPR (to safeguard the interests of the inventor/innovator) **LEADS TO** Commercialization **LEADS TO** Diffusion

Two types of innovation

1. **Incremental innovation**: Making modest improvement to existing processes/products.
2. **Radical innovation**: Creating a completely new process or product in response to a market need or opportunity; they are breakthrough innovations which can impact the entire market/industry segment.

Product and Process innovation

1. **Product innovation:** An entirely new product, which can transform the industry it is part of. Sony Walkman or Apple iPad are examples. It can also create a significantly improved version of existing product or new uses for existing product. For the innovating firm, product innovation gives the first-mover advantage and can charge high prices to yield good profits. It also uses IPR and patent to prevent/delay competition by copying.

2. **Process innovation:** It is a new/better way of making or delivering a product. Today, the Internet provides innumerable examples of process innovation. A new marketing method or organizational changes facilitating improved business practices are part of process change. Process innovation yields reduction in cost of production (by improving the efficiency of input use), enhancing product quality, and better service to customers etc.

   Some of the highly successful e-commerce/consumer Internet entities include:

   a) Amazon.com: Could well be the world's largest online store.
   b) Uber: World's largest transportation network company making available a taxi, private car or rideshare within minutes of contacting them.
   c) Airbnb: A trusted community marketplace for people to list, discover, and book unique accommodations around the world - online or from a mobile phone or tablet.
   d) Flipkart: India's most valuable e-commerce player providing online shopping options for a variety of products at the cheapest price.
   e) Snapdeal: India's largest online marketplace.
   f) Zomato India: A restaurant search platform.
   g) OLA Cabs: India's largest taxi aggregator.

From innovation to successful commercialization, a very chancy affair

The process of translating an innovation into a successful enterprise is a very challenging task. The data from US Patent &Trademark Office and the World Intellectual Property Organization indicate that in 2013 about 280,000 patents were issued in the US alone, nearly a million were issued globally but only about 10% of them will yield commercial benefits. Even if they do, the benefits won't be much. The average patent supposedly earns less money than it costs to obtain.

Chris Wasden & Mitch Wasden in their book *Tension: The Energy of Innovation* (2015), Scipio Press, Utah, USA, offer the following dispiriting numbers.

a) Only 10% of issued patents yield commercial revenues.

b) Of 1000 good ideas, only 100 will be developed into proof-of-concepts and just one will become a commercially successful product.

"Successful innovations typically follow invisible development paths and require acts of individual heroism or a heavy dose of serendipity." - Scott Anthony, David Duncan and Pontus M. A. Siran, Harvard Business Review, Dec 2014

Innovation - Summing up

Innovation can make goods and services cheaper and less resource-intensive for everyone; increase productivity and employment opportunities; save time; and enrich our lives. It is only through sustained, faster growth of innovation can any country realize faster improvement in their standards of living. One caveat to be remembered: Trying anything new is experimentation; most experimentations fail.

The mystique of entrepreneurship is that it is a subject that is not fully evolved yet to provide clear, whole answers.

5
Why Do So Many Startups Die So Young?

"Failure and entrepreneurship are natural siblings."

"Entrepreneurs are the lifeblood of any economy, and yet over 90% of new entrepreneurial ventures fail."

—**Philip Kotler, one of the greatest Management Gurus of all times**

"It is intriguing that so many ventures start in the presence of the alarmingly high rates of venture failures."

—**Mathew Hayward, Dean Shepherd and Dale Griffin,** *A Hubris Theory of Entrepreneurship*

"With all the odds against you, you need to be a little crazy to start a business."

—**Barry Moltz, a successful entrepreneur**

5.1 DEFINING BUSINESS FAILURE

"The death of a business is like the death of a loved one... the nightmare of despair and humiliation..." - **Gary Goldstick, Oregon-based management consultant**

"Business owners go through the same stages as those dealing with death: shock, denial, anger, depression and, finally, acceptance."

—**Dr. Susan Edwards, psychologist at Princeton, USA.**

Does the failure of the enterprise mean the failure of the entrepreneur in charge of it? Or, does it only mean the entrepreneur has not succeeded? There is something here beyond semantics.

There are two types of failures: Catastrophic failure and lack of success.

1. Catastrophic failures are caused by macro-economic and other factors which upset the sustainability of the business: Economic downturn; Govt. policy reversals; death of the partner; loss of a major customer; loss of key people; key supplier going bust; accidents like fire; fraud.
2. Lack of success or the business just failed. It could not succeed due to a variety of reasons including flawed decisions and actions of the promoter.

The following descriptions denote business failure, as we commonly understand:

a) Firms fail because they do not produce goods and services desired by customers at prices they are willing to pay; in short, these firms are less competitive than their rivals.

b) When there is not enough number of customers willing to buy the product at a price high enough to pay for all the inputs plus returns to investors (including the promoter) and entrepreneurial efforts. It means that an enterprise has not survived the market test, when revenues do not sufficiently exceed costs to make the enterprise sustainable.

c) When a venture becomes insolvent, it is unable to attract new debt or equity capital and, therefore, cannot continue to operate under current ownership and management.

d) Personal reasons - retirement, illness, and death of the owner or selling the business to make a profit.

e) Failure occurs if the firm fails to meet its responsibilities to the stakeholders of the firm including employees, suppliers, customers and owners.

Every business has a life span represented as a business cycle: Introduction, Growth, Maturity and Decline. Business failures could even be considered the last stage of an organization's life cycle. To some extent, such failures could be attributed to the failure of the promoter and his team to extend the life cycle through timely action.

According to the Institute of Independent Business (IIB), USA, a business failure occurs only when a firm files for some form of bankruptcy protection while others contend that there are numerous forms of "organizational death" including merger or acquisition The IIB provides the following specific criteria:

1. **Earnings criterion**: If the return on capital is significantly and consistently lower than that obtainable on similar investment.
2. **Solvency criterion**: If the owner to avoid bankruptcy or loss to creditors after such actions as execution, foreclosure or attachment, voluntarily withdraws leaving unpaid obligations.
3. **Bankruptcy criterion**: If it is deemed to be legally bankrupt. Bankruptcy is generally followed by insolvency liquidation.
4. **Loss-cutting criterion**: If the owner disposes of the firm or its assets with losses, to avoid further losses.

Jim Everett and John Watson defined business failure in terms of:

a) Bankruptcy: Discontinues operations with the resulting losses to everyone who had invested in the project including funding institutions, suppliers etc.
b) Discontinuance: Prevention of further losses; creditors might still be getting their agreed upon payments.
c) 'Making a go of it': Purely subjective reasons - mostly because of the failure of personal goals not being reached, the entrepreneur feels the efforts are too stressful or disappointing compared to the monetary and other rewards.
d) Retirement due to bad health; the enterprise hasn't failed.
e) Sale of business to realize a profit; here again, the enterprise hasn't failed.

Even an industry group as a whole becomes extinct when it is less adapted to the existing/emerging environment than a new rival group. When automobiles hit the scene, horse/bullock drawn carriages drove into their sunset.

5.2 A BUNCH OF SOBERING NUMBERS

(Most of the statistics quoted below relate to the US since it is the most researched ecosystem in the world.)

The failure rate of Startups is alarmingly high. Even in the US, with nearly the best environment for entrepreneurial ventures, the reported failure rates of new businesses during their first 3 to 5 years of operation range from 50% to 85% to 95% depending on how a business failure is defined and who is reporting it. However, what is certain is that failure is more likely to occur than success.

Dun & Bradstreet reports that businesses with fewer than 20 employees have only a 37% chance of surviving 4 years of business and only 9% chance of surviving 10 years. Of these failed businesses, only 10% close involuntarily due to bankruptcy. The remaining 90% close because the business was not successful, did not provide the level of income desired or was too much of a pain for the promoters.

As per the estimates of US Census Bureau (Business Information), over 30% of new ventures did not survive the first 2 years; 50% did not survive 4 years; 60% did not survive 6 years.

US Small Business Administration (which funds only about 5% of applicants) estimated that over 50% of small businesses fail in the first year and 95% fail within the first five years.

Of all incorporated companies, about 60% of Startups survive to age 3 and roughly 35% survive to age 10, US Bureau of Labour Statistics.

A study by Shikhar Ghosh of Harvard Business School (published in the Wall Street Journal, Sep 20, 2012) has come up with a set of findings based on analysis of data (sourced primarily from Sand Hill Econometrics) relating to a large number of Startups. These findings are at variance with the estimate of failure of 25–30% determined by the National Venture Capital Association, USA.

a) Approximately 75% of Venture Capital-backed Startups - obviously, the smartest in the Startup world - failed to return the capital to their investors, not to mention generating surpluses for themselves.

b) If failure is to be defined in terms of not meeting the financial milestones - a specific revenue growth or date of break-even on cash flow or return on investment - the failure rate is as high as 95%.

c) 30–40% ends up liquidating all assets, with investors losing all the money.

d) Many VC-backed companies are sold at a loss in a sale classified as an acquisition.

e) About 20% produce high returns.

According to Bloomberg, 8 out of 10 Startups fail within the first 18 months. The Bay Area, California, USA, has the biggest concentration of Startups and venture funding groups the world has ever known. It is home to some of the best and the brightest young minds from around the world promoting hundreds of new enterprises every year. However, the story of most of these enterprises is depressing:

a) 98% of patents never even go to market.

b) Only an estimated 0.5% to 4% of all proposals that Venture Capitalists receive are funded.

c) Each VC firm looks at about 50 plans each week, sees only 10 new entrepreneurs each week and funds only 10 deals a year. At the aggregate, VC funds look at over 500,000 proposals annually; of these about 600 become successful firms, a hit rate of a mere 0.12 %!

d) Fully 70% of VC-funded Startups fail. About three quarters of Venture-backed firms in the US do not return investors' capital.

"Most Startups fail, and most (Venture) funds fail with them." - Peter Thiel, a highly successful Venture Capitalist

Overall, enterprises not backed by VCs fail more often than VC-backed ones, typically because they do not have the capital to keep going and they cannot borrow any more on credit cards or from friends and relatives.

In the US, every year about 500,000 to 600,000 company 'births' and almost as many 'deaths' are reported. The Economist (April 16, 2011), somewhat exaggeratedly states: *Up to 90% of new businesses fail shortly after being founded; Venture Capital firms are lucky if 20% of their investments pay off.*

In the UK, out of the approximately 400,000 new businesses launched annually, one-third fail within the first three years for want of cash; another one-third could well be losing out not for want of cash but for want of customers.

About half of the new companies in Canada go out of business before their 3rd anniversary; one in four new enterprises do not survive longer than one year. For every 100 ideas that were submitted to the Canadian Innovation Centre for evaluation of their commercial potential, only 25 received favorable response. Of these 25 new project ideas, only 7 eventually reached the market place as new products, of these 7only 3 ever made a significant profit.

A recent news item quoting a study by Microsoft Accelerator gives the failure rates of Startups in India - less than half of all Startups make it past the first year and only a fifth manage to survive the third year.

5.3 WHY ARE ENTREPRENEURIAL SMEs SO PRONE TO FAILURE?

To avoid failure an entrepreneur needs to study why enterprises fail; in fact, it would be more instructive than studying success stories. SMEs in general and the innovative ones in particular tend to be more vulnerable to failure than large companies. For a Startup, to take off and fly, a million things have to align. Getting everything right from the beginning can be truly tough. Even if a Startup gets everything right, the environment it operates in turning hostile could cause the demise of the enterprise.

Most Startups try bringing a new product or a new version of an existing product to the market. When big companies introduce a new product to the market, they spend lot of time and money doing research to get everything about the new product right. Big companies have other advantages like brand power and the money to use to leverage the power and tie-ups with customers and partners. Of course, despite these advantages new products of big companies also fail. A recent study by Nielson, India revealed that only 0.14%of all FMCG (Fast Moving Consumer Goods) launches during 2012–14 (nearly 17,000) could be considered breakthrough innovations as defined by the firm in a very narrow sense. Most of the rest could have been disappointments and others total disasters.

Startups do not have much time or money to do research. So it is always a trial and error process. The smarter of them learn from their mistakes and try again. In the software industry, there is the popular concept of "pivoting". When a product fails in the market, the enterprise stops what it is doing and tries something else before the money runs out.

A typical notion around the world is that majority of new businesses will fail during their first five years of existence. It is also believed that majority of those failed could have been successful. What went wrong? Numerous factors come into play to sink businesses. It is possible that many of those failed enterprises were promoted by entrepreneurs who were not ready and able to set up and/or manage the business successfully.

The three broad types of uncertainties that entrepreneurs face are described below (oll.libertyfund.org/titles/306):

1. **Risk**: that can be measured statistically; the probability of drawing a RED ball from a jar of 5 RED balls and 5 WHITE balls.
2. **Ambiguity**: That is hard to measure statistically; the probability of drawing a RED ball from a jar containing 5 RED balls and unknown number of WHITE balls.
3. **True Uncertainty**: That is impossible to predict statistically; probability of drawing a RED ball from a jar whose number of RED balls as well as the number of other colored balls is unknown.
    a) Introducing a very novel product/service whose market doesn't exist is True Uncertainty (For instance, before the Internet, no one knew the market for Amazon, Google or Yahoo.)
    b) Even if a market already exists, there is no guarantee that a market exists for a particular new player. Even if a market exists for the new player, he still can fail to exploit the opportunity due to inadequate or ineffective planning.

To get a sense of the exceptionally wide range of challenges an entrepreneur has to grapple with, it is helpful to study business failures in terms of causes that are under the control of the entrepreneur and those beyond him. Also, there are inherent disadvantages of being small.

An entrepreneur can contain, if not avoid, venture failures by managing known causes of failure, which are under his control. The owner-manager is the most critical decision-maker for the small enterprises. Hence, the destiny of the enterprise is greatly determined by the promoter's traits, competencies and commitment. In fact, his inadequate level of understanding of the management practices driving business success do account for a significant proportion of business failures.

FACTORS WITHIN THE CONTROL OF THE ENTREPRENEUR

Entrepreneur-centric Factors

1. **Strong ego, over-optimism, over-confidence**
   a) Ego blinds him to recognizing signals of impending problems and seeking and accepting suggestions.
   b) Entrepreneurs tend to be overly optimistic about the chances of their business. (After all, they would not otherwise be in business!). It is not that entrepreneurs are wholly unaware of the fact that most ventures fail. But they believe that they can beat the odds. They disregard challenges, ignore the downside and, thereby, failing to have a fallback plan if the assumptions are flawed or his efforts fail. The over-confident and overly enthused entrepreneur over-estimates market potential and under-estimates competition, project cost and completion time.
   c) Obstinacy: Sticking-to-your-vision approach may not work for Startups. You may need to revise your original ideas several times in light of new insights about emerging market conditions or Government policy changes or other factors.

2. **Burning out:** Startup founders may not have the luxury of trying to achieve work-life balance. Some, therefore, run the risk of burning out. Some others can, of course, be lackadaisical; not giving the enterprise 100% of time and efforts; not working hard enough or fast enough or smart enough.

3. Not infrequently, a personalized, even **autocratic management style** devoid of delegation stifles enthusiasm and pro-active participation in innovative initiatives by partners or employees. Lack of trust and openness and disinclination on the part of the owner-manager to share business information and strategic plans with those who are part of the enterprise can be counter-productive.

4. **Living beyond the means that can be supported by the business**
5. **The promoter falls in love with the product**: The benefit of professional decisions can be derived only by being totally detached and unsentimental.
6. **Some promoters mistake a business for hobby:** Just because you love something doesn't mean you should convert it into a business. Research your business idea thoroughly to ensure that it is viable.
7. "**Poor fit**" between the promoter and the chosen venture; the mismatch between the demands of the project and the competencies or inclinations of the owner. The business owner has no business being in the business he is in. "Good fit" is a function of consciously exploring the right fit. It could, in fact, be a matter of luck as well.
8. **Limited or no network**: *"Your network is your net worth"*. Those who succeed fully harness their professional and personal connections for a range of support.

Deficient Overall Management

1. **Having the wrong founding team, having the right team, which breaks up too soon, or no team at all.**
   a) Single founder can avoid the problems a team may cause, but seldom works. *"Even if you can do all the work yourself, you need colleagues to brainstorm with, to talk you out of stupid decisions and to cheer you up when things go wrong".*
   b) Inability to keep the founding team together: founders falling apart can, at times, be fatal. As Noam Wasserman says in the book *Founder's Dilemmas*, "It's unfortunate but true: If entrepreneurship is a battle, most casualties stem from friendly fire or self-inflicted wounds". The problems within Startup management teams are considered to account for 65% of failures within the portfolio companies of Venture Capitalists. Great companies achieved greatness because the founders had faith in each other till the companies stabilize their operations. An outstanding example is the unbreakable alliance of the original promoters of Infosys Ltd., India long enough for the company to become a solid, world-beating champion.

c) **'Mousetrap' Teams:** Even if the best mousetrap is developed by a group of brilliant technologists, the world may not beat a path to their door if they had no exposure to the process of commercializing technology. None of them may have much insight into what consumers are looking for in a solution to a given problem or what the competition offers as a solution.

2. **Picking the wrong idea/product:** Imitation of some existing successful business is surely one of the options, but need not be the best option. Choice of the wrong idea reflects inadequate efforts to choose the right idea.

3. **Absence of a viable business model:** A business model describes a plan to bring in more revenue than expenses.

4. **Poor project planning and execution** can cause the downfall of a Startup even if the idea is clever. Inadequate competencies of the project team generally explain sluggish execution. The consequences include:

    a) Cost/time overrun.

    b) Inability to deliver expected benefits.

    c) Negative market perceptions and loss of customers.

    d) Weak supplier relationships.

    e) Talent flight - losing smart employees.

5. **Bad location of the project:** Inadequate availability of the required infrastructural and support services and difficulties of optimizing the logistics of transport of inputs and outputs will adversely affect the economics of the project.

6. **Choice of inappropriate technology and scale of operation**

7. **Hiring the wrong people or hiring too many people upfront**

8. Setting goals is essential but **setting unworkable or unrealistic goals** can be self-defeating.

9. **Poor systems of control to measure performance** - quantity and quality of production, production costs, financial parameters etc. - spell trouble.

Deficient Marketing

1. **Building a solution without a problem**: Find the customers first, and then look for solutions; *"build it and they will come"* approach won't work.

2. According to Paul Graham, the co-founder of Y-Combinator, a highly successful US-based Business Incubator (which provides physical facilities, mentoring and other services), Startups flop because they run out of money. **They run out of money because either they fail to make something people want or they fail to sell what they produce.**

3. **Not defining the target market:** Failing to design the product to meet the needs of the target customer group; not getting the attention of prospective customers and not converting them to customers.

4. **Over-estimating market potential/under-estimating competition**: Inadequate knowledge of customer needs and inadequate understanding of the strengths of competition.

5. **Over-dependence on a single customer**: Losing the customer would mean closing up shop.

6. **Failing by scaling**: A serious mistake Startups tend to make is to scale (expand) without understanding what it takes to support 100 customers vs. 10 customers. That is, scaling prematurely without carefully assessing the resources - staff, leadership, infrastructure, systems, and funds - to be mobilized to achieve controlled growth. Going after all the business you can get drains your cash and reduces the overall profitability. You may have to incur large upfront costs to finance large inventories to meet new customer demand. If the overall demand falls, loan repayment will be a serious issue. Slow and steady wins all the time. One of the best barometers for scaling should be consumer satisfaction. If your consumers are satisfied and they want more, you can scale as fast as you want.

7. **Timing failure:** You can be late in the market and face well-entrenched competition. In some instances, you can be too early and the market is not ready yet for your particular solution because the consumers are happy with what they have; the time and cost to

be invested to attract enough number of customers may add up to something beyond what has been planned.

8. **Picking a niche that is too small**
9. **Lack of competitive advantage:** No clear product differentiation/positioning: It is easy to start me-too kind of businesses because of their simplicity and relatively low capital requirement. However, lack of competitive advantages makes them extremely exposed to new entrants (even existing competitors) who could cut prices to the bone to wean customers away from you.
10. **Poor pricing strategy:** *"Pricing is one part science, ten part art. And a dark art..."*
    a) Too high a price can put off prospective customers; too low a price may generate low net surpluses.
    b) The common practice of cost-plus pricing without considering how prospective customers perceive the value your product delivers could lead to under pricing (when the consumers are willing to pay more than the price you set) or over-pricing (which the market will not bear).
11. **Competing head-to-head with industry leaders:** Entrenched market leaders with deep pockets can destroy the chances of small enterprises.
12. **Poor product quality:** *Dogs don't eat your dog food!*

Flawed Financial Planning

1. **Raising too little money to take off:** Underestimating the amount of time and capital necessary to reach cash flow break-even.
2. **Raising too much of capital** and investing in inessential items. When you have too much capital, it could cover up internal weaknesses for some time.
3. **Too much leverage:** Both financial (debt) and operating (fixed overhead costs) burden.
4. **Poor cash management:** Running out of cash, being very optimistic about the market acceptance of the product, revenue stream, on the one hand, and over-spending on the other. When you are a Startup,

suppliers require immediate/quick payment for inventory. If you sell your product on credit, the time between making the sale and getting paid can be months.

5. **Personal use of business funds**

FACTORS BEYOND THE CONTROL OF THE ENTREPRENEUR

1. Overall economic conditions turning bad
2. Competition from a new source; new product based on new technology. To some extent, this could be due to the failure of being alert to market developments.
3. Possible risks within the industry: Health (e.g. Maggi imbroglio in India), safety and environmental risks
4. Your major supplier goes bust
5. Demand for the product falls; a key consumer cancels orders
6. Adverse government policy changes
7. Squeeze on credit facility; consumer finance shrinkage

5.4 DISADVANTAGES OF BEING SMALL

1. Closure rates of small businesses, particularly Startups, are much higher than those of larger firms. Lenders, therefore, tend to be very cautious about lending to SMEs. Further, SMEs have very limited collaterals in relation to their borrowing needs. This phenomenon encourages lenders to charge higher rates of interest to offset their risk perceptions. In countries like India, Government policies enjoin banking institutions to provide loans to SMEs at rates of interest even lower than the prevailing market rates.
2. Small businesses with limited capital cannot hope to enter value-added manufacturing services or industries. Financing upfront costs becomes difficult. Whereas success in many cases is conditional to financing upfront costs of installing new machines, in addition to the upfront development or marketing costs.
3. Small businesses often fail because of insufficient management know-how and professionalism that in turn lead to the absence of right system of controls to manage organizational activities.

4. The size precludes task specialization, which helps enhance operational efficiency and reduce direct costs. Most functions are integrated or highly concentrated, with the "owner-manager occupying the roles of composer, conductor and sometimes even performer".

5. Inadequacy of overall internal resources acts as a drag on dedicating sufficient efforts to innovation and new product development. Most may not have a strategy to respond to changing environments. For small businesses, the concept of strategic planning may seem not so relevant or too complicated to get a handle on. They seem to ignore the Darwinian dictum: *"It is not the smartest, nor the strongest that survive, but the most responsive"*.

6. Small businesses tend to focus on survival, pre-occupied with immediate issues; likely to be very action-oriented with little time to think through or reflect on larger issues or long-term goals; possibility of "ready, fire, aim" mindset setting in.

Scale effect

a) Being denied the economies of scale arising from the size of operation; larger the plant, lower the cost per unit of output because, for one thing, the fixed costs get distributed among larger number of units of output.

b) They don't enjoy suppliers' discounts for those placing large orders (available to large enterprises); small businesses, therefore, pay higher unit price for inputs.

c) Difficulties to respond to market opportunities in terms of meeting the requirements of large volumes and standards; limited exposure to international markets. Constraints of market intelligence, credit, scale economies, quality, reputation etc. make exporting disproportionately difficult for many small enterprises.

Experience effect

Greater experience leads to labour efficiency, work specialization, innovative production processes, product standardization, quality control and other performance-boosting factors. Startups do not have this benefit.

Other factors

a) Inability, due essentially to high costs, to acquire such support services as training and skill development, logistics and market intelligence; professional consultants not equipped with appropriate cost-effective management solutions for the scale of small enterprises.

b) Regulatory compliances: Cumbersome entry difficulties and administrative barriers imposing relatively high costs including management time, a very scarce resource.

c) Globalization enhancing business risks associated with uncertainty, the flip side of the opportunities globalization is unlocking.

d) Lack of direct access to capital markets for upgrading existing facility or for growth.

e) Limited access to policy makers.

f) Insufficient supply of skilled workers.

g) Difficulties in acquiring better quality raw materials.

h) Difficulties of leveraging efficient distribution channels largely controlled by large firms.

i) Sustained growth is essential for stability and survival. This calls for continually fine-tuning product range and quality, developing new distribution models, scaling up etc. This process necessitates bringing in more funds and attracting professional talents. Small enterprises have difficulties in meeting these pre-conditions.

5.5 THE FORGOTTEN MIDDLE

Most of the debates on SMEs relate either to the few insanely successful or the majority that fall by the wayside. There is a large group of SMEs that is stuck in the middle.

1. Neither have they performed well enough to be rated as successful nor have they done so poorly that they are forced to close down.

2. They are the 'living or walking dead', still living and breathing enough for the enterprise to keep going although they may not be going anywhere.

3. They ended up where they are because of several causes:

a) They could have unwittingly committed a mistake: The prime promoter choosing the wrong partner, choosing the wrong technology, locking themselves into the wrong customer group, hiring the wrong people, any of which could handicap the business severely.

b) Unwillingness to close shop: Some refuse to see the writing on the wall and continue to run the business as if there is no alternative.

c) Promoters' life priorities undergoing a transformation: After achieving a certain level of material success they reset the priorities thereby weakening the business drive and risk-taking motivations.

Enterprises also fail by being at the wrong place at the wrong time - bad luck!

A US Bank Study on why businesses fail
(www.usbank.com)

Three major reasons: Bad management, bad financial planning and bad marketing

1. **Bad management**
   a) Over 75% of the businesses failures studied lacked a well-developed Business Plan; the business owner's limited understanding of the business he is in.
   b) Over 70% of the businesses surveyed were managed by hugely optimistic (using "rose-colored calculators") entrepreneurs who over-estimated revenue and under-estimated cost.
   c) About 70% of the failed businesses were led by entrepreneurs who were in denial regarding their own competence or incompetence; never bothered to seek assistance
   d) Over 60% of the businesses that died due to bad management were led by promoters with no relevant or applicable business experience.

2. **Bad financial planning**
   a) Over 80% of the business failures reported poor cash flow management

b) Close to 80% of the businesses were inadequately funded to begin with
   c) 75% miscalculated the cost of doing business.
3. **Bad marketing**
   a) Close to 65% of the businesses studied died due to bad marketing: Either minimized the importance of marketing and promotion or ignored it totally
   b) 55% of dead businesses either didn't even know who their competition was or chose to ignore it
   c) Close to 50% of the deceased businesses relied on just one or two customers for the bulk of the revenues. When even one goes away, so does most of their revenue.

Case Study: The Story of Friendster and Facebook

Both Friendster and Facebook were social media sites with the same mission to increase interactivity between users on their respective websites. While Facebook became a game-changing, world-beating entity, Friendster, the pioneer, failed to sustain its early success.

Friendster launched earlier to the general public in 2003, acclaimed the first successful social network website. It made $13 million at the end of the first year. Facebook opened its doors in April 2006. By end 2008, its turnover was $272 million. Friendster started floundering and dissolved its website by mid-2011.

What went wrong or right?

1. **Flouting a cardinal principle of a social network's success**: Easy navigation. MySpace of Friendster became a blotted nightmare so difficult to navigate; Facebook was simpler.
2. **Lack of development/not keeping up with the times**: Willingness and ability to change and keeping up with competition are essential ingredients for success. Facebook adapted readily by building News Feed (to ensure Facebook users did not need to navigate away to other sites), opening up its site to third party developers and constantly added new ways of interacting with friends allowing the visitors to attach links, videos or posts to a "wall" which friends could see. Friendster's response was inadequate.

3. **Listening to the market**: Facebook was in development for a couple of years before it was released to everyone online. Businesses and schools around the world were invited to use the social network and allowed Facebook to test their systems and improve features, adapting to meet the demands of the users. Friendster became complacent not inventing new ways to engage its users.

4. **Taking risks**: Friendster had an advantage in being the first major social network and could have built an unchallengeable lead on its rivals if it had taken more risks with its interface, design and overall features. Facebook kept on taking risks even with its winning formula, keeping its users engaged and improving functionality.

5.6 FAILURE OF ENTERPRISES: A NATURAL PHENOMENON?

Possibility of failure stalks most enterprises, small or big, most of the time. Entrepreneurs walk a very fine line between embracing failure and winning the game because they are compelled to continually make choices between unsatisfactory alternatives, under conditions of huge uncertainties. More often than not, such decisions are based on inadequate information.

a) Risk-taking in the absence of adequate knowledge and a realistic assessment of the probabilities of different outcomes comes pretty close to gambling.

b) Even when you have all the information, the decision you take today may yield results tomorrow counter to what you thought they should be. Because, the contexts keep changing. **In the entrepreneurial world, no problem seems to have a satisfactory solution, no solution lasts long.**

Businesses seldom, if ever, function as planned. They are 'living and breathing' organizations that undergo frequent changes, responding to changes in the real world. The real world has its own logic, reason and pace as it evolves itself. Clearly, an individual entrepreneur is subject to the dynamics of the real world with unpredictable outcomes.

A sampler of the unending chain of choices to be evaluated to decide which ones to be acted upon is presented below:

1. Product and its features
2. The target market and its characteristics
3. The partners: Can't live with them, can't live without them!
4. Technology and innovation: From concept to commercialization; from mind to market; technology determines the life span of an enterprise
5. The location
6. The plant size
7. Choosing the right equipment configuration
8. How much to make in-house, how much to be outsourced
9. Money and control: Owning a little of a lot or a lot of a little; 10% of one making Rs. 100 million or 100% of a company making Rs. 10 million
10. Building the right team
11. Should decisions be intuitive or analytical? How does one make the right decisions?
12. How important is doing the right thing (being ethical) to an entrepreneur?
13. Family business: Sons and daughters, survival and succession
14. Harvest/exit strategy: Is growth good or bad? And how will one know? Nobody knows for sure when to keep going and how long and when to quit.

Even with the best of efforts, things could still fall apart due to external factors. In many such cases, the entrepreneur could neither have anticipated what is coming nor could he have insulated the venture against the ill effects of such external forces.

5.7 FAILURE AS A PRE-REQUISITE FOR SUCCESS

We are obsessed with being successful. Expectation of an endless vista of success is indeed unreasonable. No matter how diligently we plan, something always goes wrong. In fact, the very fear of failure makes us commit mistakes, which naturally increase the odds of failure.

Total failure is surely unacceptable. But some degree of failure could be viewed as a learning process. Beneath the surface of many great business successes, one could find a trail of failures that was part of their story. Two of the most celebrated creators of high-tech products of our times, Steve Jobs and Bill Gates, had to live with so many product failures.

Steve Jobs' failures

Ever heard of: Newton Message Pad? Portable Macintosh? Apple Pippin (a gaming system)? eMate 300 (low-cost Laptop)? Macintosh TV? Lisa - Personal Computer ? iPod U2? Power Mac Cube (a Lucite box)?

All of these were Jobs' failures. Jobs' failure after failure taught him lessons to become a winner. Jobs failed better than anyone in corporate America.

Bill Gates' failures

1. First company, Traf-O-Data was a failure. The project was for manufacturing a machine to process/analyze traffic-flow data. Gates and his partner Paul Allen spent 2 years and US$1500 in the making of it; spent 6 years in trying to sell it. The end result was net losses of US $3494 before closing it.
2. The database called Omega, which the company spent 5 years to perfect, was abandoned.
3. When he introduced Windows 1.0, it was a failure. After a few years later, after putting more money into re-development it was introduced as Windows 2.0. That didn't work either. But Bill Gates didn't give up. He interacted with customers and learned more and then introduced Windows 3.0 which was a huge success.
4. After sinking millions of dollars and countless hours of developer time, the project to jointly build OS/2 with IBM was cancelled.
5. "Microsoft at Work", a project to revolutionize office machines such as copiers and faxes, was canned because it never worked!
6. Zune, the MP3 player, was a dud.

Paul Allen, Gates' associate, said, *"Every failure contains the seeds of your next success. The lessons learned provided the keystone for the creation of Microsoft."*

3M Corporation succeeded mainly because the mistakes and failed efforts during the different stages of the growth of the company did not discourage it from pursuing their goals.

Even big guys failed to the point of bankruptcy before finding their success. Founders of companies like De Lorean Automobiles, General Motors (much, much before the company collapsed into Government's arms in 2009), 20th Century Fox Film, Heinz, Hershey's and entrepreneurs like Walt Disney, Henry Ford, Charles Goodyear and Donald Trump are examples.

Teflon, Dynamite, Velcro, Cellophane and Post-it-Notes are examples of "failure" becoming highly successful products.

Innovations by new firms (releasing better quality - more durable - product or a product with larger functionalities or a cheaper product or a product which is more environment-friendly or a product based on renewable materials or…) kill existing enterprises even if there is "life left in them". Of course, that is a bad thing for the promoters who own and manage such enterprises; at least, initially. But for the society at large it could well be a good idea. This is the concept of "**creative destruction**" defined by Joseph Schumpeter: An inherently non-viable enterprise to be closed down at the earliest to minimize further losses and the resources thus saved to be reinvested in sounder business opportunities.

In light of the above interpretation, we need to review our perspectives about success and failure. All business closures need not necessarily represent 'failures' in any meaningful sense; many were 'successful' at closure.

LEARNING FROM FAILURE

"It's fine to celebrate success but it is more important to heed the lessons of failure."

—Bill Gates

Future success of a 'failed' entrepreneur depends on an honest assessment of what went wrong and how to make it right and how to avoid making the same mistake twice. Identify your mistakes and ask what could have been done better. The key is in discovering what was in your control and what wasn't.

To reemphasize, what makes Silicon Valley, USA successful as the engine of high-tech growth is the

Darwinian process of failure. As author Mike Malone put it: *"Outsiders think of Silicon Valley as a success, but it is, in truth, a graveyard. Failure is Silicon Valley's greatest strength. Every failed product or enterprise is a lesson stored in the collective memory. We don't stigmatize failure; we admire it. Venture Capitalists like to see a little failure in the resume of entrepreneurs."*

Here is another passionate proponent of failure!

"The Silicon Valley of today is built less atop the spires of earlier triumphs than upon the rubble of earlier debacles... Failure is the safety valve, the destructive renewing force that frees up people, ideas and capital and recombines them, creating new revolution... Failure is what fuels and renews this place. Failure is the foundation for innovation." - Paul Saffo, *Failure is the Best Medicine*, Newsweek, March 25, 2002

The motto should be: *"Ever Tried. Ever Failed. No Matter: Try Again. Fail Again. Fail Better."*

QUOTES ON LEARNING FROM FAILURE

"Anyone who has never made a mistake has never tried anything new."
—**Albert Einstein**

"Our greatest glory is not in never falling, but in rising every time we fall."
—**Confucius**

"As soon as I stop failing, I have stopped trying to innovate."
—**Adam McFarland,** a successful entrepreneur

"Success is a lousy teacher. It seduces smart people into thinking they can't lose."
—**Bill Gates**

"The fastest way to succeed is to double your failure rate"... "Failure is a harsh teacher, but the best"
—**Thomas Watson Sr.** (Founder of IBM)

"If you are not failing every now and again, it's a sign you are not doing anything very innovative."

—Woody Allen, Hollywood director

"The biggest successes are often bred from failures."

—Randif Kemisar,
Consulting Professor of Entrepreneurship
at Stanford University

Thomas Edison tried over 10,000 different experiments before he demonstrated the first incandescent light bulb on 21 Oct 1879, *"I have not failed. I've just found 10,000 ways that won't work."*

"I missed more than 9000 shots in my career. I have lost almost 300 games... I have failed over and over again in my life. And that is why I succeed."

—Michael Jordan,
one of the greatest basketball players.

"Each failure taught me so much. Success teaches you nothing."

—James Dyson
(He re-invented the vacuum cleaner; during close to 5 years he created 5127 prototypes to refine the design)

"Invariably we try ten things that don't work out in order to do one thing that is successful. And we learned a lot in doing the ten things that didn't quite work."

—Larry Page (Co-founder of Google)

6
Entrepreneurial Success: Beating the Odds

A Startup faces nearly impossible odds. Success is exceedingly rare, as the reported rates of failure have amply demonstrated in the previous chapter. Entrepreneurial success must, therefore, be studied, celebrated and treasured.

Determinants of Entrepreneurial Success - A Primer

1. Promoter's personality traits
2. Promoter's entrepreneurial insights
   a) Choosing the right partner
   b) Choosing the right business, delivering new value to the customer
3. Promoter's managerial competencies
   d) Having a comprehensive plan incorporating the key project components
   e) Mobilizing required funds
   f) Assembling the right team
   g) Smart execution
   h) Close monitoring
4. Serendipity/luck: Being at the right place at the right time

6.1 DEFINING ENTREPRENEURIAL SUCCESS

"Success is a journey, not a destination" - Ben Sweetland, author of *Grow rich while you sleep*

"*Entrepreneurial success is intensely personal. It is not pursuit of an outcome. It is a process of continually beating challenges. For the true entrepreneur there is no arrival, only continuance"* - Peter Baskville, Founder of Skillmaker.edu.au

Entrepreneurial success denotes a somewhat complex blend of a compelling consumer need, a winning solution and a sustainable business model. What scales to use to gauge the success of an enterprise? Quantitative measurements of performance in relation to competition are extensively deployed because of their relative ease of application.

1. Size-oriented: Number of employees, sales, investment, plant capacity etc.
2. Growth-oriented: Sales, profit, employees
3. Profit-oriented: ROI, IRR, ROA etc.

A set of personal, sociological and environmental factors are at play during the process when an enterprise is born. Three important factors help achieve business success: The opportunity, the entrepreneur and the resources needed to start the business.

Entrepreneurial performance has traditionally been examined in terms of two sets of factors:

1. Entrepreneur-centric attributes like his traits or personality characteristics and competencies that contribute to the success or failure of his enterprise
2. A set of project related circumstances and the environment it operates in which contain the seeds of success or failure.

In both cases, the entrepreneur has to face the underlying challenges: If he does not have the traits, he must acquire them (not an easy proposition) or partner with someone who has them. To exploit the opportunities, the potential entrepreneur should acquire the required resources, design appropriate strategies reflecting environmental realities and execute the project effectively.

Winning is not merely "not losing". To sustain the winning streak, the winner has to:

1. Avoid the foolish things the loser did.
2. Do things more smartly such smart things the loser did.
3. Do exceptionally smart things that the loser may not even be aware of.

6.2 THE INEXPLICABILITY OF ENTREPRENEURIAL SUCCESS

"Astonishingly, as important as these companies are to the economy, no one - - not even the most-respected academics or well-heeled venture capitalists - - knows what it takes to intentionally design and create high-growth, scalable successes." - Kauffman Thoughtbook 2011

The path to business success has been described as, simply *"... you make some stuff, sell it for more than it costs you... that's all there is except for a few million details. The devil is in those details!"* - Ben Botes and John Vinturella in the book *Release Your Inner Entrepreneur.*

As stated earlier, an entrepreneur has to get an astoundingly large number of complex things right: Partnerships, product selection, scale of operation, technology, location of the business, manufacturing operation, make or buy decisions, personnel, financing, market segmentation, pricing, promotion, timing and managing the environment

For even the greatest management Guru, taking on the role of a prophet predicting how a given enterprise will perform even in the short-term can turn out to be a professionally mortifying experience for more than one reason.

Isolating all the known factors that affect the performance of an enterprise and assessing their effects do not yield reliable results most of the time. Because there could still be residual set of factors, mostly beyond the control of the entrepreneur, which are unpredictable, unknown or even unknowable.

The factors that made a specific enterprise in a specific location successful may not be strictly relevant to another enterprise in another location. Likewise, the conditions that made an enterprise successful in a specific year may not be applicable to another enterprise in another year.

Statistically, the chances of lasting in business for a minimum number of years may not be high. Those having the benefits of strong business experience and expertise of the founding team, careful planning and smart execution have a greater chance of success than those who could not marshal such strengths.

Some achieve success by diligently conforming to the received wisdom on conceptualizing, planning, executing and managing enterprises. A few others tear through the revered practices of the day and do radically different things, pursuing possibilities which few thought existed. (According to Sam Walton, the celebrated promoter of Wal-Mart, one of the world's biggest companies, the most important rule in business is to break all rules). A tiny proportion of the rule-breaking entrepreneurs become winners. Most of the rest fail, no matter what they do. This explains the enduring mystery of entrepreneurship.

Part of the problem is that most of management science is not truly a science governed by irrefutable rules. Many management principles are nothing more than "wet fingers in the wind" (The Economist, Oct 24, 2009); sailors in ancient times depended on this simple method to determine the direction/force of the wind. Management science is essentially about individuals or groups of individuals representing themselves or an organization trying to get the best out of a given situation - - a promoter seeking to maximize surplus, an intermediary brokering a deal looking for a win-win situation, a consumer wanting to get the best value for money or a company striving to maximize shareholder value.

Behavioural economists have, in recent times, been demonstrating that human behaviour is far too complex to yield easily usable postulates. The Economist referred to above quotes a rigorous statistical analysis of the performance of some of the much-ballyhooed companies; the study concluded that luck was just as plausible an explanation of their success as excellence.

The entrepreneurs know that all those who succeed nearly always did it right. The irony, however, is that not all who did it right will always succeed; something called 'luck' is a constant ingredient. Regardless, they must continue the journey with the conviction that *"their time will come"*.

Entrepreneurial success is not a straight path. Despite failures and disappointments, the driven entrepreneurs press ahead, propelled by the inner drive, the tenacity and the passion to win. Many successful enterprises demonstrate that the gains from the success will exceed the losses from many failures. Apparently, it is this assurance that drives entrepreneurs.

In fact, motivated entrepreneurs are racked by the fear of not trying. Even if the chances of success are slim, they will try. As pointed out earlier, they look at failure as an opportunity to learn.

The authors are not claiming that a wide range of insights, processes and practices that have been brought together on how best to plan, execute and manage an enterprise, if acted upon, will guarantee success. But then, those who are not Bill Gates' or Steve Jobs' following the tested and proven principles and practices is infinitely smarter than trying to be Bill Gates or Steve Jobs!

6.3 THE DRIVERS OF SUCCESS

"Success comes from good judgment. Good judgment comes from experience. And experience often comes from bad judgment!" - Bruce Dunlevie, Venture Capitalist

"... The magic ingredient for entrepreneurial success is an unreasonably bloody-minded determination to keep going come hell or high water!" - The Economist, Oct 2012

An enterprise is a collection of tangible and intangible "assets": Plant and machinery, people and their skill sets, financial resources, patents/technology, reputation and good relationships with customers and suppliers of inputs. The success of an enterprise depends on how effectively these "assets" are taken advantage of.

The key drivers are:

1. Promoter's personality traits and competencies
2. Rigorous analysis and planning
3. Flawless execution
4. Close monitoring
5. Continuous review by revisiting all key assumptions: Many problems arise from "applying perfectly sound judgment to wrong assumptions."
6. Continually recalibrating all vital processes
7. Laser-like focus on the customer

There are no magic solutions or one "right" formula which will guarantee a business success; nor does exist any reliable predictive cause-effect model. It's all about addressing ever-changing needs of the customer by continuous improvement of organizational performance by enhancing organizational agility and productivity.

The study of human skills and resources and how they are leveraged in an enabling environment, which facilitates the process, provides some clues to the understanding of entrepreneurial success.

PROMOTER'S PERSONALITY TRAITS

(See detailed discussion on the subject in Section 3.6)

"... The so called 'successful entrepreneur' is an elusive, many - splendored beast ... the ten easiest bosses to work for, and the ten most difficult bosses to work for; bleeding heart liberals and tough libertarians and shades in between all build thriving firms; firms succeed by being bold and brash and churning in change and also by being narrowly focused and conservative and extremely understated in their strategies; both formal strategic planning and lack of it seem to have worked." - **Saras D. Saraswathy, faculty, Darden School of Business**

Success is the tenacity of the inner motivation of the promoter. Brooke R. Envick, a prolific analyst of entrepreneurship, has identified two major sets of skills of the entrepreneur contributing to the success of an enterprise:

1. **Psychological Capital**: An array of personal characteristics - self-esteem, hope, optimism, confidence, willpower, resilience, motivations etc. We can also add on creativity; the important resources that contribute to entrepreneurial creativity are motivation, personality, thinking style, intelligence and knowledge.

2. **Social Capital**: Who the entrepreneur knows and what networks he is associated with, his reputation and credibility in the community; networks help derive the benefits of accessing resources (talents/finance), information and reduced transaction costs.

"Building a Startup is all about building credibility – with investors, partners, customers, the media."

—**Daan Weddepohl, Founder of Peerby.com**

Some analysts believe that the determination of a promoter to launch an enterprise or not giving up what has been launched arises from two great motivations of entrepreneurial achievement: Love and fear.

a) Many successful entrepreneurs start their venture by doing something they love. Jeff Bezos loved books and then launched Amazon.com. *"It is the satisfaction of doing it for yourself and motivating others to work with you in bringing it about. It is about the fun, innovation, creativity with the rewards being far greater than purely financial."* - Richard Branson, Virgin brand of companies

b) Fear factors impelling not to give up include possibility of bankruptcy, having to flout financial covenants, losing key people and losing face.

The characteristics of a successful entrepreneur as defined by Herb Kelleher, co-founder & CEO of Southwest Airlines are *"reasonable intelligence, good health, optimistic disposition, lengthy attention span, perseverance and a love of people."*

Those who succeed keep an open mind, listening to their customers, their people, associates, mentors etc.

PROMOTER'S MANAGERIAL COMPETENCE/EXPERIENCE

Role of human capital in entrepreneurial success is widely recognized. Those owners with higher human capital are more efficient in managing enterprises than those with lower human capital. A spectrum of attributes signifies human capital: Startup experience, management experience, industry experience, opportunity recognition skills, organization skills, leadership skills, and formal education.

Not only the promoter but also the employees have to have appropriate skills, abilities, knowledge and experience.

To conclude, the skills and competencies necessary for being successful in business are those which help:

a) Discover and develop new products
b) Market the products of quality at appropriate price consistently and reliably
c) Make a profit

RIGOROUS RESEARCH AND PLANNING

"… A genius is often merely a talented person who has done all of his or her homework." - **Thomas Edison**

Startups or SMEs in general simply do not have the luxury of making mistakes of investing the time, money and effort of the promoter in an activity which doesn't fly. Even if you have a highly rated original concept, the chances of success are small. Careful planning is the key. Tools and processes for evaluating the strengths and weaknesses or the commercial viability of a project are increasingly getting sophisticated with proven rates of success.

The important goals of the planning process are:

a) Making an accurate assessment of target customers and the emerging market conditions. (See details in Market Feasibility in Chapter 7.2, Part II).

b) Assessing the technical viability of the investment proposal (See details in Technical Feasibility in Chapter 18, Part V).

c) Having a careful assessment of the financial requirements of the project and the financial viability analysis. It takes money to make money. One has to know what one has, what one needs and what needs to be done (See details in How Best to Manage Money in Chapter 9, Part II).

d) Developing the best and the worst-case scenarios to help anticipate the range of adversities that can hit your company and plan for appropriate responses.

e) Preparing a Business Plan incorporating the important techno-commercial aspects of the project.

Success is seldom, if ever, an accident; successful businesses are seldom taken by surprises. Anticipating the likely changes in the business environment and readying the enterprise to deal with such changes – positive or negative – improve the chance of success.

HAVING A *'DEVIL'S ADVOCATE'*

A *'Devil's Advocate'* plays a healthy role by presenting plausible, alternative explanations of observed phenomena.

A small group of professionals having no stake in the project should be asked to question/test all assumptions relating to all major decisions. The most desirable thing is to test how many of the promoter's assumptions might be wrong. Experienced professionals as Mentors or as Members on the Board play this role for young Startups. The prime promoter/founding team can, thereby, free himself/itself from 'confirmation bias' – not looking for ways to confirm that the promoter is right.

ADAPT OR PERISH

"It is neither the strongest species that survive, nor the most intelligent but the ones most responsive to change."

—Charles Darwin

Accept that change is inevitable or unstoppable and mostly irreversible. Adapt to rapidly changing circumstances better than your competitors should be the *mantra* for survival. Rapid change, like most things in business, is a threat but also an opportunity.

Adapting effectively begins with a sound understanding of business conditions, where they are headed to and the key trends in demographics, technology, economics, consumer behaviour, government policies, finance, trade etc.

Keep a close watch on competition. If your enterprise is losing ground in product quality, service, image, consumer satisfaction, unit costs and profitability in comparison with competitors, it means they are adapting better. Continually monitor and upgrade the organizational structure of the enterprise to promote initiative, innovation and performance.

LOOK FOR WARNING SIGNALS

Failure is a process. It is not as if the business owner wakes up on a fine morning with a sick business which was healthy when he went to sleep. The most frequently used metaphor, in this context, is the one relating to the frog and hot water. Throw a frog into a tub of hot water and it will try mightily to get out as fast as it can. But if one were to turn up the heat slowly, the frog will in time get boiled without realizing what is happening.

One must always be alert to warning signals such as: Falling even stagnant sales with falling gross profit margin, decreasing market share, rising inventories, rising Accounts Receivables, increasing customer complaints, non-payment to suppliers, declining employee morale, falling reserves and investments, and banks getting tougher.

SOME ANECDOTAL PROPOSITIONS

Entrepreneurs with previous Startup experience are more likely to be successful in their new Startup attempt. Such experience provides the relevant Social Capital – network etc. The greatest benefit is that the mistakes made earlier could be avoided.

Having parents who set up and managed a successful enterprise increases the likelihood for someone to set up his own business for the obvious reason that this background gives the confidence that entrepreneurship is a viable career option.

RANKING OF SUCCESS FACTORS

Based on a survey of 685 entrepreneurs, Ernst & Young published a document in 2011, *Nature or Nurture: Decoding the DNA of the Entrepreneur*. The ranking of success factors to the question, *"What specific forms of education or sources of learning provided you with the skills needed to build successful businesses?"* was as follows:

Experience as employee: 33%; Higher education: 30%; Mentors: 26%; Family: 21%; Co-founders: 16%; Secondary education: 13%; Colleagues: 12%; Friends: 11%; and Investors: 5%

6.4 SUCCESS, A CAUTIONARY TALE

Success may be simply meeting the demand by supply at the right moment, in the right amount at the right price. Sustaining success, however, requires unrelenting passion and focus, continuous learning, unlearning, relearning, information and analytical intelligence, confident foresight on technology and market and the right support and funding.

Nearly always, entrepreneurial success and the resultant organizational expansion give rise to hierarchy, bureaucracy and complacency. These outcomes can collectively kill the entrepreneurial spirit, which triggered the success in the first place. Continually asking such questions as – what can go wrong? How can I prevent it? What did go wrong? How can I fix it? – would help fine-tune strategic interventions to stay ahead.

Business growth and success is a double-edged weapon. Problems strike at the moment of high growth.

You will have to hire more people, acquire new machinery, expand the factory, using up accumulated cash and, therefore, requiring additional cash infusion. This can create more liabilities, unless, of course, the financials of the enterprise are strong.

"Every success sows the seeds of failure. Success is intoxicating and addictive. It makes us arrogant. We become myopic and ignore changes that don't suit us."

—Ashok Gupta, Mid-American Journal of Business

Those who extol business success cannot totally ignore the line of critique arising from what is known as "survivorship bias"-this statistical reasoning solely on the basis of the lessons learned from winners, ignoring the lessons yielded by the losers the number of whom could well be several times that of the winners.

No matter what the reasons are, there will always be more failures than successes of entrepreneurial ventures. However, the successes have been of sufficient number and their impact quite impressive that they continue to contribute to economic advancement by creating new innovations, new products, new industries, new jobs and new competencies or skill sets. This actuality provides the undying fascination for pursuing entrepreneurship as a career by a few who dare to dream big and make it and indeed by a much larger number who want to make a living.

> **CASE STUDY: Nordic region's entrepreneurial renaissance**
>
> The society at large in the region is increasingly enthusiastic about creating a holistic ecosystem – funding, incubation, policy support etc. – to promote and sustain as many Startups in as wide a range of activities as possible. All are convinced that Startups alone can generate quality jobs on a scale warranted. The governments are creating agencies to promote Startups, encouraging Universities to commercialize their ideas and promote Startups and telling their schools to sing the praises of entrepreneurship!

a) Finland is becoming the champion in the region. The Startup Sauna – a Business Incubator run by young professionals, now being funded by the government, business and academia – is a case in point. Like all such Business Incubators/Accelerators, it offers a wide range of services, working space, coaching for budding entrepreneurs, study trips to Silicon Valley and plenty of networking opportunities.

b) Finland is home to a vast number of Startups including 300 founded by former Nokia employees. The Startups are amazingly wide-ranging:

   i. House-cleaning business: Convincing companies to use the services as a reward for their employees and free them from domestic tasks; persuading the government to treat house cleaning as a tax-deductible benefit;

   ii. Delivering bags containing all the ingredients needed for a meal, chopped and ready to cook, copying IKEA's do-it-yourself model; and

   iii. A device that lifts wintry dark moods by shooting bright light into the ear canal.

CASE STUDY: Why Israel the hotbed of entrepreneurship

The blurb of the book, START–UP NATION The Story of Israel's Economic Miracle, claims it "*addresses the trillion-dollar question: How is that Israel - a country of 7.1 million people, only sixty years old, surrounded by enemies, in a constant state of war since its founding, with no natural resources - produces more Startup companies than large, peaceful and stable nations like Japan, India, Korea, Canada and the United Kingdom? Israel's adversity driven culture fosters a unique combination of innovative and entrepreneurial intensity.*"

Israel (accounting for less than 3% of US population) produces the second largest number of Startups per year in the world, next to USA. Israel has more companies on the NASDAQ (the second-largest stock exchange by market capitalization in the world, with heavy representation of technology-related companies) than those from all of Europe, Korea, Japan, Singapore, China and India combined.

There is a collection of enabling factors, which makes Israel so innovative and entrepreneurial. *"... It consists of the tight proximity of great Universities, large companies, Startups and the ecosystem that connects them - including everything from suppliers and engineering talent pool and venture capital... The role of the military in pumping R&D funds into cutting-edge systems and elite technological units and the spillover from this substantial investment, both in technologies and human resource, into the civilian economy."*

Then, of course, *"... is a cultural core built on a rich stew of aggressiveness and team orientation, on isolation and connectedness and on being small and aiming high."*

The Economist (March 14, 2009) argues that young Israelites conscripted at 18 learn the virtues of teamwork and improvisation. Many start businesses with friends that they met in the army. *"Add to that a high tolerance of risk, born of a long history and an ever-present danger of attack, and you have the makings of an entrepreneurial firecracker."*

Exceptional human capital - highest ratio of PhDs per person, the highest ratio of engineers and scientists and some of the world's best research Universities - has surely been the key enabler.

CASE STUDY: How does Amish Community win business?

The US-based Amish are one of the most insular communities anywhere. They don't drive cars or use electricity or phones in their homes. They leave school after 8th grade. They are known for their plain life styles marked by simplicity and bound by strong work ethics - *"I would never ask an employee to do something that I wouldn't be willing to do myself."*

"The failure rate of Amish businesses is less than 10% in the first 5 years as compared with 50% of small businesses in the rest of the US over the same period. " - TIME Magazine, April 19, 2010

Such a high success rate is explained in terms of a disciplined work ethic which emphasizes frugality, thrift and humility.

Strange indeed are the ways of entrepreneurship!

6.5 LUCK/SERENDIPITY

Every business requires a little bit of luck to be successful; could well be a matter of timing – being at the right place at the right time. But then, how is that some people keep getting lucky over and over again? May be, their smart actions improve their luck.

What do successful entrepreneurs attribute their success to?

"Member of the lucky sperm club" ... *"a winner of the ovarian lottery"*

—Warren Buffett,
one of the smartest investors of all times

"Incredible planetary alignment... half luck, half good timing and the rest brains."

—Jeff Bezos,
Founder of Amazon, world's largest e-commerce company

"Was lucky to be born with certain skills."

—Bill Gates

Serendipity is a more credible argument. Many analysts attribute Steve Jobs' successes to the good fortune of being born at the right time lived at the right place. He grew up in Mountain View and Los Altos during the 1970's. With the invention of the microprocessor and the development of Internet, Silicon Valley was agog with technical ideas and versatile components and sub-systems waiting to be converted into mass-market product possibilities. Jobs saw the opportunity and seized it fast and intelligently.

Of course, many as brilliant as Jobs could have sensed the possibilities. But then, one has to be an entrepreneurial genius (which Jobs surely was) to ride the high tide of product revolutions.

"Silicon Valley is obsessed with serendipity... (A term) long referred to a fortunate accidental discovery... Today serendipity is regarded as close to creativity -- the mysterious means by which new ideas enter the world.", Greg Lindsay, New York Times, Apr 5, 2013

Google attributes the genesis of innovations like Gmail, Google News and Street View to professionals having unintended, chance conversations on the corridors or in the cafeteria. Google's new campus has buildings resembling bent rectangles to facilitate "casual collisions of the workforce"!

PART II
Winning the Battle for Survival

7
How Winners Win Customer Loyalty

"Business is not about creating products. It's about creating consumers."

—Peter Drucker

7.1 LASER-LIKE FOCUS ON CUSTOMER

We may be stating the obvious or over-simplifying a vital business function. However, we have to make a set of observations to put our propositions in perspective:

1. Your business exists only because you have 'enough' customers who are willing to buy your product at a price you set because your product:
   a) Delivers real or perceived value to them, which is higher than the price they pay.
   b) Offers better value for money than what competition provides.
2. The growth of your business, by consistently winning and retaining customer loyalty, is a function of:
   a) Increase in the number of customers.
   b) Increase in the average value of purchase.
   c) Increase in the frequency of purchase.
3. People buy to satisfy basic needs or to solve a problem or to make themselves feel good. For consumer products, the relative value consumers get includes financial benefits – lower cost of acquisition, installation and maintenance – and non-financial benefits like security, health, well-being, status etc.
4. Businesses buy to maintain operations or to improve revenue or to reduce expenses or to improve productivity.

5. For some industrial products, especially those with high unit value, it may be worthwhile presenting a simple cost-benefit or return on investment analysis – how customers could get a payback on their investment within so many months/years as a result of using your offering.

6. Customers, in fact, don't buy your product! What they buy is the solution to a problem or the fulfillment of a need. When customers buy an antiseptic product, what they buy is freedom from worrying about infection and germs. You are, therefore, not selling your product but selling the benefits embodied in the product.

7. It is increasingly being acknowledged that the surest way to improve profit and gain competitive advantage is by providing positive customer experience both at the point of sale and after the sale.

8. Because all customers may not be equally profitable (the surplus of revenue earned over the costs of making and delivering the product), customer-centric approach focuses on the most valuable customers to make sure they are happy. Products and services are specifically designed around the needs of high-quality customers who stay loyal to your enterprise, with low attrition rate.

9. Customers are becoming more demanding, more selective. You have to be absolutely customer-focused to provide solutions to ever-changing consumer needs. For designing the right product for the right customer group, the first step is to rigorously study the potential customers to get to know them thoroughly, the problem the customers want to solve or the outcome they want to achieve.

DEFINING YOUR CUSTOMER AND THE CUSTOMER NEEDS

"The more you know about your customers, the more you know about your company. Customers tell you how to succeed in market place." - Paul Tiffany, Steven D. Peterson, Colin Barrow, *Business Plans for Dummies*

Profiling your consumers in terms of common, identifiable characteristics and, hence, similar requirements/problems which your product can take care of is the beginning of the process. Customers can be thought of in terms of:

a) Individuals and families, institutions like public agencies, corporates, NGOs etc.

b) Location: Local/regional/national/international.

c) Primary basis of buying decisions: Price/quality/service/convenience/others.

d) Periodicity of buying the product: Daily/weekly/monthly/annual/on-demand.

e) Channels being used and their location.

Customer group representing individuals is primarily defined in terms of demography. Demographic indicators include age group, sex, level of education, occupation, level of income, marital status, type of traveling, urban/rural etc. Customers can also be defined in terms of Psychographic (attitude, personality, motivations to buy etc.) and Socio-graphic (membership in clubs, professional association, recreation, hobbies etc.) indicators.

If the customer is a business entity or other institutions:

a) Get a sense of the organization in terms of annual income, number of employees, annual purchases of the product you offer.

b) Arrive at the consumption norm of the product similar to what you propose to supply in relation to the business unit's output. For instance, a car tire manufacturer may assume five tires per car to get at the total demand from car manufacturers.

c) Level at which purchase decision is made.

d) Key factors impacting purchase decision - price, quality, warranty, reputation etc.

Closely observing the behaviour of the customers to know what is on top of their minds is an essential step. Ask them the right questions. (Let us ignore the story about Henry Ford who was supposed to have said *"If I had asked people what they wanted, they'd have said faster horses!"*) Potential customers must be part of the "solution" and be involved in the process.

What do they want and cannot buy? What do they buy and don't like? Where do they buy, when and how? What are they buying more of? If your product would do such and such, would they be interested? How interested? At what price?

The above process helps define your target market segment. This segment represents those consumers who are most likely to buy your product because the 'solution' that you offer matches precisely what they are looking for.

A compelling customer value proposition should emanate from the above analytical process. Such a proposition will provide details of the benefits the customers owning your product will derive.

If you want your potential customers to switch from their existing suppliers, you have to provide a credible answer to the question why and how what you offer is better than what competition does. In other words, you have to clearly **differentiate** your product from that of competition. After all, if the quality and price of your product are the same or close to that of competition why would people want to switch?

The superiority of your product (to what your competitors offer) could be in terms of: Lower prices; higher quality; lower cost of installation and maintenance; greater convenience; greater reliability; wider functionality and product features; faster delivery; smarter aesthetic appeal; more prompt after-sales services (Superior service could by itself be an important differentiator for customer loyalty and retention); longer warranty or any other unique attribute that your competitors cannot easily duplicate

In sum, a business can deliver 3 core types of value to the customer:

1. Low cost achieved through operational efficiency.
2. Top quality product by getting everything right–advanced process technology, manufacturing excellence, superior quality inputs etc.
3. Delighting the customers with the aid of outstanding services.

You have to create the value and communicate it to your present and prospective customers. One great example of this is what Apple communicated to its customers - *"By using iPod, our customers will feel the joy of having 1000 songs in his/her pocket and listening to them wherever they are."* Your business succeeds only if a certain minimum number of customers recognize the value of your product and are willing to pay for it.

7.2 MARKET FEASIBILITY : ASSESSING THE MARKET POTENTIAL

The laws of supply and demand determine how much an enterprise can sell and, more important, at what price which may determine the commercial success of your project. This analysis has to be set against the backdrop of the status of the industry the product is part of: Is it growing or shrinking? Even if not growing, are there promising niches within that? In general, what are the opportunities and threats?

Estimating the current and potential size of the market for your product is estimating the number of consumers who have the need for your product and who will buy your product when they have other options to meet their needs; that is, there could be competing products or even substitutes. Market potential is forecasted within a range to take into account the upside and downside of market trends.

How much you can sell is also determined by the existing and emerging competition. Hence, a competitive/competitor analysis is part of this exercise.

The best information creates the best decisions. The data requirements for such analysis are met through collecting and analyzing secondary data (published information) and primary data that are to be collected from the market through direct mail, telemarketing or personal interviews, with varying costs and benefits.

BARRIERS TO MARKET ENTRY

What barriers to entry do you face in the target market and how do you propose to get over them? Some such barriers are:

a) Well-entrenched existing competition.

b) High marketing costs.

c) Consumer acceptance and brand recognition.

d) Difficulties of breaking into the distribution network controlled by big players.

e) Need for key partnerships with suppliers and customer groups and expert management team.

f) Unique technology and patents and product superiority which competitors possess.

g) Switching costs for customers to accommodate your product.

7.3 TARGETING NICHE MARKETS

(www.smetoolkit.org is the main source of the following discussion on niching)

Customer-centric efforts will generate only limited rewards if you are looking at the 'wrong' customers in relation to your offering. At any point in time, even in matured markets, there are opportunities, niches or small group of consumers with potential, if you deliberately look for such opportunities. Niche is a portion of the market in which you have a unique advantage; a small corner largely overlooked or under-exploited by the competitors because it is too small for big players. It can provide adequate revenue for a young, lean enterprise.

Small firms have to be creative in launching new business concepts. They have, after all, only limited resources – physical, human and financial – to manipulate the overall market structure or to finance aggressive competitive actions against bigger rivals in the market. To survive and prosper, they should take the time to identify the niche in which they are most likely to succeed and identify the resources required to exploit the opportunities.

You start with small exploratory forays into easy-to-enter market niches and use the experiences gained to build competencies to conquer more challenging and profitable market segments that you keep identifying as you proceed.

Niche markets are generally local markets or a small number of customers with specialized needs. A niche player tries to become a specialist in its chosen area and will pursue either cost advantage or some form of differentiation within the segment. Look for specific niches, which are currently:

a) Not fully served or served at all - they don't get what they want.
b) Not satisfied with what they get: The product offering of existing players do not meet the needs of the consumer; there must be a better way of satisfying the need.
c) Not being offered adequate choices.
d) Being over-charged by existing suppliers.

Such a situation could emerge because:

1. There are not enough suppliers to a specific field.
2. Such suppliers as exist are too slow to respond to changing market requirements.
3. Poor reputation for quality or outmoded product features.
4. Indifferent customer service.
5. Irregular product supply to the market or slow delivery.
6. Bigger firms have ignored the segments.

Small firms can/do survive by picking market segments which are not particularly quality conscious and can do with products with less features, thereby, reducing the overall cost. Lower costs, lower performance initially, but gets better over time. For instance, there is a growing market in India for, say, machine tools for small and medium-sized general engineering units, a segment mostly catered to by suppliers from the State of Punjab. In the US context, such companies as General Motors, Ford, Eastman Kodak, HP and Microsoft started off in niches.

ADVANTAGES OF NICHING

The enterprise's capturing of a greater proportion of the sub-segmented market results in less competition and greater profits since niche customers tend to be less price-sensitive. The enterprise does not have to face powerful rivals.

By zeroing in on its very best business prospects from the beginning, the company's marketing investment can yield a higher return. The business costs of winning and retaining customers tend to be lower. Word-of-mouth marketing occurs much faster and customers are easier to identify and access. Initial investment in R&D or in manufacturing facilities or for working capital will be limited. Niche-centric customers tend to be loyal, if they are effectively taken care of.

Once you have built one successful niche and understood the underlying process, you could as well build a similar business that serves a somewhat different niche or add more products/services to more profitably serve the existing niche – "cross-over niching."

RISKS OF PURSUING NICHE MARKET

In business there are no certainties or guarantees. Even playing in the smaller pool comes with its own sets of risks. It is estimated that only about 10% of all businesses are niche-focused.

Many entrepreneurs believe that niche-centric approach will limit their opportunities. Depending solely on a narrow customer base can turn out to be risky; having the flexibility to take on new ideas is essential for survival. Hence, they target demographic markets with huge populations.

Once an enterprise is known for one thing, moving too far from its specialty may encourage customers to shift their loyalty.

It is possible that the bigger rival can enter the same market niche and supply a similar product to that offered by the SME. And by using its deep pockets, it can finance aggressive competitive actions against the SME and grab the market niche.

7.4 THREE POPULAR MARKETING CONCEPTS

UNIQUE SELLING PROPOSITION (USP)

An USP is an exclusive or differentiating aspect of your product that may even define your business. Differentiating your product from the competition helps your product stand out and command premium-pricing capability.

Your USP must paint a mental picture. Look at your product from the point of view of a customer. Ask yourself, "If you were in the market for buying the product your business is trying to sell, what would you look for? What aspects of the product will compel you to buy?" Look at your competitors and find the strong characteristics of your product that differ from those of competition and highlight them.

The differentiation could be in terms of price, wider functionality, customization, speed of service, greater convenience, greater reliability, smarter aesthetic appeal, quality or any other unique thing your competition cannot easily duplicate.

CUSTOMER RELATIONSHIP MANAGEMENT (CRM)

The latest *avatar* of customer-focused initiative comes under CRM. Customer retention through customer loyalty is just about as important as customer acquisition. In fact, it is cheaper to retain a customer than to get a new one. Emerging as a key element of the corporate strategy, it has arisen from the clear recognition that long-term relationships with customers are one of the most important assets of an organization.

Information Technology is an effective tool to facilitate customer ownership. You must assemble a database, CRM System and e-mail marketing programme to communicate with your customers regularly. IT enables managing the data to understand customers so that the right CRM strategies can be adopted. To improve customer retention, three main steps are required:

1. Customer retention measurement
2. Identification of root causes of defection and related service issues (customer dissatisfaction)
3. Development of corrective action to improve retention

Enterprises are finding linkages between employee satisfaction, employee retention, customer satisfaction, customer retention, sales and profitability.

SUSTAINABLE COMPETITIVE ADVANTAGE (SCA)

No discussion on winning customers and, therefore, business can end anymore without referring to SCA. All enterprises – big or small, low-tech or high-tech, young or old, belonging to consumer goods segment or capital goods segment – have to ensure that their competitiveness remains intact.

Even if you are the first person to launch a specific product, there is no guarantee that you will be the one who ultimately benefit from the opportunity discovered. Someone else who is better positioned can reap the rewards of the market that you have created. It is your SCA that can ensure that you do not lose out.

SCA is a collection of distinctive tangible as well as intangible capabilities, which cannot easily be imitated or innovated around by existing or new competition. It distinguishes your product from your competition.

Broadly the capabilities will cover technical, financial, marketing, explicit knowledge, non-exclusive licenses, IPRs, exclusive licenses etc. Intangible capabilities include strong brands, leadership, tacit knowledge and skill-sets, teamwork, organizational culture, business processes and partnerships.

There is a range of strategic as well as tactical options for differentiating your product. (This discussion partly overlaps with that on USP) The "uniqueness" of a product could well be physical or even psychological. Broadly a firm can differentiate its product from that of competition in 4 ways:

1. Physical and quality superiority: Features, performance, durability, reliability, ease of installations and maintenance and style.
2. Services/support differentiation: Delivery, installation, customer training, consulting services, maintenance and repair etc.
3. People superiority: Includes competence, courtesy, credibility, reliability, responsiveness and communication skills.
4. Having a superior brand image.

By being a specialist is another option:

a) Custom specialist: Creates customized products to order.
b) Quality/price specialist: Concentrates on the low or high end of the market.
c) Service specialist: Offers one or more services not available from other firms.
d) Product-feature specialist: Produces only a certain type of product or product feature.
e) Geographic specialist: Sells only in a particular geographical area.
f) Specific customer specialist: Sells only to a few major customers.

7.5 LEAN STARTUP

Eric Ries, Harvard Business School Entrepreneur-in-Residence and the author of *The Lean Startup*, suggests a customer-centric strategy for business success. The idea is launching as quickly as possible a minimum viable product, a bare-bones creation that includes just enough features to allow for useful feedback from early adopters. Such a product will be followed by many product upgrades incorporating new insights from the customers and others. In other words, an effective solution for the needs of the customers is created with the help of consumer feedback on the first version of the product (This process is essentially applicable to software industry and services in general. Conventional manufacturing units do not have such flexibility).

This approach *"favors experimentation over elaborate planning, customer feedback over intuition and iterative design over traditional 'big design upfront' development."*

7.6 COMPETITIVE/COMPETITOR ANALYSIS

Does the potential customer already have solutions to the need/problem you have identified? If so, what are they?

How loyal are your potential customers to their current suppliers?

What are the shortcomings of current suppliers? Does the customer perceive these shortcomings? What are you planning to do differently from what your competition is doing?

What are the main benefits for users of your offering which you can persuasively communicate to prospective customers?

Is the existing/emerging competition manageable?

In order to identify opportunities and threats and uniquely position your product, you have to analyze competition on the basis of their strengths and weaknesses relative to your own. The range of parameters that are relevant while doing competitive analysis includes:

a) Product quality; features and options; range and variety; reliability and durability; fit and finish and aesthetics; retained value; ease of maintenance and repair; frequency of follow-ons.

b) Strength of process technology

c) Scale of operation

d) Marketing budget, pricing, distribution, advertising and sales promotion, credit policies

e) Customer services, customer loyalty and brand awareness.

f) Financial stamina.

g) People skills and retention.

h) Strategic alliances with suppliers, customers etc.

i) R&D investment.

j) Environmental responsibility.

k) Political leverage.

(For an SME some of the parameters referred to above may not be as important as for large firms)

7.7 MARKETING STRATEGY AND PLAN

The core of the marketing strategy and plan represents tailoring the product offering and its pricing, distribution and promotion to suit the demands of the target segments more effectively than competition.

You have to have an appropriate strategy to win, a strategy/plan which is continually updated to respond to changing environment.

Entrepreneurs and managers are often so pre-occupied with immediate issues that they tend to lose sight of the long-term priorities and goals. A strategy for growth provides an effective framework for making informed decisions, a clear plan of action. Strategic thinking helps determine how the market will evolve into the future and how the enterprise should be positioned to benefit from the new market dynamics.

Where are we? Where are we going? How will we get there?

Strategic plan, a living document, is about differentiating how your business satisfies customers, how your business acquires competitive advantage by differentiating itself through a wide range of tools: Pricing, product-mix, choice of distribution channels, packaging, and promotion.

Strategic plan attempts to align the available or acquirable strengths of the enterprise to available or potential opportunities. To do this effectively, you need to collect, screen and analyze data/information about the business environment.

Marketing experts strongly recommend that the best strategy for SMEs is to compete on a 'variable' cost basis rather than on a 'fixed' cost basis. Given their small size, they cannot enjoy the benefits of economies of scale and, hence, there is no point in expanding the capacity by investing in capital equipment to reduce unit cost of goods sold. There is so little scope for volume sales. When facing difficult market conditions, the less fixed costs you have to support, the more survivable will your business be. (Of course, if the market for your product grows beyond your existing capacity, you expand your capacity).

One of the operational strategies small enterprises resort to, when confronting the conventional marketing of large companies with superior resources, is "guerilla marketing" using the weapons of speed, mobility and flexibility.

PRICING DYNAMICS

Pricing is essentially based on marketing factors: Demand and supply, competitive position and perceived value. The 'right' price attracts and retains customers and, at the same time, generates adequate net surplus. Every product has a threshold price level. Higher price than competition is to be justified in terms of such merits as newness, quality, warranty, service etc. Lower price than competition and to maintain profitability you have to have efficient manufacturing and distribution and/or lower cost of raw materials, labour, overhead etc.

You need to be clear whether you are targeting a high-end customer or a low-end, budget customer? You can be the best or the cheapest; you can't be both.

a) If you are targeting the high-end customer, low prices may be interpreted as cheap and low quality.

b) If you are targeting a price-sensitive segment, your prices have to be low and competitive.

Determining an optimal price is not a one-off affair. Taking into account how the product performs at a given price and responding to marketing situation, you re-price your product at regular intervals.

A well-chosen price will do three things:

1. Achieve the financial goals of the firm.
2. Conform to market conditions – will the customers buy at that price?
3. Support a product's positioning (luxury category, middle-income, low-end) and be consistent with other variables in the marketing - mix like distribution and promotion.

DISTRIBUTION

How do you propose to reach your customers? Convenience of the customer to acquire your product is the first concern; optimizing the cost of reaching the product to the customer through the different channels is another goal. The latter has to be achieved while keeping intact the incentive of the different channels to stock and promote your product.

Each product group has to choose the appropriate channel strategy. The options available are retail, wholesale, agencies, independent representatives and distributors. Some reach their customers directly through own sales force or otherwise. Internet is yet another option to interact with customers; e-commerce is growing in the country at a pace one could never have imagined before.

ADVERTISING AND SALES PROMOTION

Communication with existing and potential consumers and other stakeholders like trade, employees and investors is vital for a firm's success. The communication or promotional strategy is aimed at:

a) Providing information about the product to prospective customers to persuade and influence a favourable customer decision.

b) Differentiating the product of one's enterprise from that of the competition by communicating to consumers meaningful distinctions about the attributes of a given product. The attributes could include price, quality and usage. Market research helps identify what consumers want and what attributes are important to them.

c) Reassuring buyers that they have made the best purchase decision. This customer conviction enhances the product's value, creates an enduring brand image and strengthens loyalty to the brand or firm.

d) Stimulating sales amongst former, present and future consumers being the ultimate goal.

The promotion mix consists of four basic elements: Advertising, Sales Promotion, Direct Marketing or Personal Selling and Publicity.

Advertising

Advertising is a means of communication with present as well as potential customers to generate in them such enablers as awareness, knowledge, liking, preference and conviction which could lead to purchase. The objective of advertising is to inform, persuade, remind and reinforce.

The advertising strategy must determine the budget, the message, choice of media for delivering the message and the measurement of effectiveness of the campaign.

Advertising media include print media – newspapers and magazines – radio, TV, Cinema and outdoor media/hoardings. The new media, especially Internet-driven ones, are increasingly becoming popular. Web banner ads, web popup ads, mobile advertising and e-mail advertising are examples.

The size of the advertising budget will determine the composition of advertisement mix and the frequency of release of advertisement. The choice of media depends on the media habits of prospective customers – readership, viewership etc. – and, of course, the reach of the media.

Sales Promotion

Sales Promotion consists of various incentives, mostly short-term, intended to stimulate quicker and/or larger purchase of a product by end-user or intermediate distributors/retailers. They reward the existing customers or increase the consumption of occasional users.

Sales Promotion activities include trade shows, contests, displays, free samples, point-of-sales promotion and offering two-for-the-purchase-of-one. They tend to be time-specific.

Direct Marketing

Direct Marketing involves face-to-face interaction/selling with prospective customers for making presentations, answering questions and procuring orders; direct mail; catalogue distribution; and telemarketing.

DIGITAL MARKETING

Given its innate merits – cost effectiveness, target orientation and result-driven – digital marketing today enjoys worldwide popularity. Of course, this is irrelevant to product categories targeting low-income consumers without any access to anything electronics. Digital marketing is one of the cheapest platforms for reaching out to the maximum present and potential customers, for promoting visibility and for getting feedback from the customers to continually improve the product offering.

Facebook and Twitter campaigns and pay-per-click campaigns on Google along with search engine optimization help enterprises and their products get noticed within the shortest time. MSMEs can list their products for direct sales on e-commerce stores like Amazon and e-bay.

A good Social Media strategy will help even MSMEs position their products and enterprises in the best possible light at the lowest cost.

7.8 WHAT DOES THE MARKETING GURU SAY?

Even the best of strategies need not necessarily yield returns you look for. You only get narrow windows of opportunities. Philips Kotler's observations are patently pessimistic. According to him, marketing strategies are showing diminishing returns:

1. Product differentiation is harder to achieve.
2. Mergers & acquisitions have as many failures as successes.
3. Internationalization is offering fewer opportunities: Either the good markets are overcrowded or the poor markets have no money.
4. New products fail more times than they succeed.
5. Price cutting doesn't work because competition will match.
6. Price raising doesn't work since there isn't enough differentiation to support it.
7. Cost cutting has eliminated much of the fat but now risks cutting the muscle.

7.9 TIMING IS EVERYTHING FOR SUCCESS

For new products to succeed, a bunch of enablers have to be in place. For example, the idea of human flight had fascinated men forever. It is argued that the Wright Brothers didn't win because they were smarter or worked harder or luckier than Leonardo da Vinci. They won because their efforts occurred 4 centuries later.

To give another example: Tablet computing failed for years and years. Then, Apple succeeds with its iPad. That Steve Jobs was a genius doesn't alone explain the success. His genius, in fact, was waiting for the required advances in multi-touch screens and related user interfaces, low-power processors and wireless broadband and then striking as soon as these elements were available at a reasonable cost.

7.10 SOME CHARACTERISTICS OF NOT-SO-ATTRACTIVE MARKETS (www.ic.gc.ca)

1. **Highly competitive market**: Contains numerous, strong or aggressive competitors, characterized by price wars, advertising battles and new product introductions.

2. **Threat of new entrants**: An industry will be unprofitable if the entry barriers are not high enough to discourage new entrants who can bring in new capacity, new technology, and substantial resources.

3. **Threat of substitute products**: Substitutes can limit the profit potential of an industry by placing a ceiling on the prices it can charge.

4. **Strong bargaining power of the buyers**: Price-sensitive buyers can lower profits by containing prices or demanding higher quality or more services. When buyers are organized or concentrated or what they buy accounts for a large portion of their costs (of operation) or the industry product is undifferentiated or the buyers' cost of switching suppliers is low, such a situation can emerge.

5. **Strong bargaining power of suppliers**: An industry is unattractive if its suppliers have strong bargaining power that can squeeze profits out of an industry by raising prices or reducing the quality or quantity of ordered goods.

8
How Best to Manage Partners & Employees

Businesses, small or large, live or die on the choices made during the process of decision-making by the promoter/leadership, managers and others at all levels. Businesses survive and flourish when the leadership, managers and other employees learn to make better choices in a given context.

8.1 MANAGING PARTNERS/CO-PROMOTERS

No enterprise can be a solo act. In fact, a typical enterprise is not an individual but a team (More than half of US entrepreneurs share ownership in their business Startups). The odds of one person having a wide range of skills for launching and managing an enterprise are slim. Obviously, you have to forge partnerships with individuals or have a strategic alliance with an institutional entity. Leveraging the skills of partners can be beneficial to all. Of course, you also have to hire professionals with the right competencies to manage the enterprise.

Choosing the right partner: All partners are not created equal! Some partners will make you whereas others can break you. Choose the one with integrity, appropriate experience and a commitment to collaborate.

A clear partnership agreement is essential to sustain partnerships:

a) Keeping personal relationships and business relationships independent of each other.
b) Defining personal goals and long-term business goals to avoid conflicts.
c) Sharing profits in a pre-determined proportion.
d) Dealing with disagreements; a mechanism to resolve them.
e) Having a plan to deal with the situation when a partnership is broken for whatever reason.

8.2 MANAGING EMPLOYEES

"It is the magic of a team that transforms into a vital enterprise."

Founders are certainly the life during the early stages of an enterprise; later a strong professional team with appropriate skills and experience is vital. So is a clear and mutually agreed definition of the roles and responsibilities of each member.

Your professional team is the most important predictor of success of your enterprise. Most successful entrepreneurs readily agree that the asset base of an enterprise is to be defined in terms of the knowledge, creativity, commitment and capacity to collaborate of each employee. Attracting, retaining and empowering professionals with the complementary talents and skills will, therefore, represent the most critical task.

a) In fact, successful entrepreneurs have no problem recruiting professionals smarter than themselves for a specific function or even for overall management. Because, a smart team can be a competitive business advantage. Making the members of the team collaborate and excel in their performance that ensures synergy, an outcome that exceeds the sum of individual contributions, should be a cardinal goal of every enterprise.

b) Ideally, the management team has to have the same incentives as the founder/founders. Putting 15–20% of the company into the hands of your employees (Employee Stock Option) will be motivating and loyalty instilling.

Employees are to be treated as customers, internal customers. Maximizing value delivered to these customers pre-supposes:

a) Careful, fair, transparent selection process.

b) Initial as well as on-going training programmes.

c) Setting measurable and attainable goals, assigning specific actions with responsibilities and completion dates and rewarding employees for achieving goals.

d) Delegating responsibility and authority to your team: No matter how smart you are, it is a mistake to try to do everything yourself. You focus on things that you do best.

e) Providing leadership by the promoter: Coaching, mentoring, motivating, inspiring, empowering and committing the team to contribute their best to achieve the goals of the organization.

f) Competitive, performance-based rewards.

g) Career growth programmes.

h) Helping those who don't measure up to find other opportunities.

Ensuring a safe, caring, structured and non-discriminating workplace provides the best chance for improved employee commitment leading to higher levels of loyalty and better performance for the business.

According to Alexander Kjerulf, an international consultant on making the workplace a happy place, happy companies are more efficient and make more money because they have: Higher productivity; higher quality; lower absenteeism; less stress and burnout; the best people; higher sales; higher customer satisfaction; more creativity and innovation and more adaptability.

For SMEs, scope for such elaborate or structured formats of practices is limited. Given the small size of the organization, the relationships between the promoter and his employees tend to be less formal and more intimate. However, it must be of the highest priority that the employees feel strongly committed to the enterprise; such a commitment can arise only if they feel that their destiny and that of the enterprise are inextricably bound together.

---

13 practices for managing people

(Jeffrey Pfeffer, Professor of Organizational Behavior at Stanford University)

1. *Employment security: long-term commitment by the organization to its workforce*
2. *Selectivity in recruiting*
3. *High wages*
4. *Incentive pay: Sharing in better performance and profitability*
5. *Employee ownership (Employee Stock Options)*
6. *Information sharing*

7. *Participation & empowerment: Decentralization of decision making and broader worker participation*
8. *Self-managed team: Teams are responsible for hiring, purchasing, job assignments and production thereby reducing management levels/layers.*
9. *Training & skill development.*
10. *Cross-utilization & cross training: Having people do multiple jobs have benefits, making work more interesting.*
11. *Symbolic egalitarianism: Comparative equality; no executive dining room, everyone eats in the same cafeteria; wears similar smock, no reserved places in the employee parking lot.*
12. *Wage compression: Not only in terms of hierarchical compression (CEO pay relative to that of others), but also horizontal wage compression; reduces interpersonal competition.*
13. *Promotion from within.*

9
How Best to Manage Money

9.1 THE SIGNIFICANCE OF SOUND FINANCIAL MANAGEMENT

Every business decision - whether hiring an employee or raising the commission to the trade or buying a new computer system - is a financial decision because each decision has a financial impact. All successful businesses follow strong financial management practices; all those that practice good financial management are more likely to succeed than fail.

This causality is particularly strong for SMEs for which an unpaid invoice could well precipitate the risk of insolvency.

In the UK, about 400,000 new businesses are launched annually. One-third of them fail within 3 years, not for want of customers but for want of cash.

Dun & Bradstreet estimates that more than 80% of small business failures in Australia could be attributed to bad financial management – poor cash flow, debtors out of control, chasing revenue growth without focusing on profit margins and overtrading beyond the business's ability to meet commitments.

There is, therefore, a direct correlation between the quality of financial management and small business financial health. Understanding one's finances and financial statements is fundamental to assessing what a business needs to survive and grow. Continuously tracking financial metrics – profitability, cash flow cycle, working capital requirements, available liquid assets, credit to fund operations and expansion etc. – and taking appropriate actions determine business success.

9.1.1 Money is not your friend

If you are too conservative with your cash, you will not be able to make the investments and take the calculated risks to grow your business.

Whereas being careless with money is also an enterprise – killer. If you don't know the difference between 'spending' and 'investing' (or don't do the latter well), you are likely to end up wasting money with nothing to show.

Not having enough money is a perennial problem facing most MSMEs. If you don't have enough money to launch your business and fund it for, say, 3 years until the enterprise finds itself on firm footing before takeoff, you are going to make poor choices.

9.2 FUNDING REQUIREMENTS

Different phases – implementation phase, growth phase, and maturity phase – of the business life cycle have different financial requirements.

A very careful assessment of the funds requirement is the first step. How much money do you have? How much you need to live on? How much does the business need? How will you raise the money you require? What are the relative costs of funds from the different sources? Definite answers to these questions have to be found before you take the first step for starting a business.

Funds are required to meet a variety of expenses:

1. **Preliminary and Pre-operative Expenses**: Preparation of feasibility studies, company formation, salary and other expenses of professionals recruited for overseeing the implementation of the project until it starts generating revenue, interest to be paid (during the implementation phase) on loans taken and, of course, the promoter's salary and other business-related expenses.

2. **Costs of acquiring the fixed and other assets**: Land and land development, buildings, machinery, process technology, office equipment etc.

3. **Margin money for Working Capital**: A certain portion of the Working Capital has to be funded by long-term capital, the rest being funded by the commercial banks as an on-going activity.

4. **Provision for contingencies**

The above four sets of requirements of funds have to be funded by Equity and Loan; in some cases Government grants and subsidies supplement the funds.

Equity is essentially brought in by the promoters and their associates; other sources are institutional investors like State Industrial Development Corporations or other State agencies dedicated to providing financial assistance to specific categories of entrepreneurs, Venture Capital and Angel Investors. New enterprises have, of course, the option to go for a Public Issue as and when ready.

Loan Capital is obtained from institutions like Industrial Development Corporations, State Finance Corporations and Commercial Banks. Selling Bonds or other debt instruments and leasing are other options.

Short-term trade credit by suppliers of equipment or raw materials and upfront payment by customers represent other small contributions.

9.3 DETERMINING FINANCIAL VIABILITY

An investment proposal is a stream of costs/expenses and a stream of benefits/incomes. Minimizing the costs and maximizing the benefits are the twin tasks. Further, the surplus of benefits over costs should be large enough to make the investment in a given project worthwhile. Would the investor be better off investing in the proposed business rather than leaving the money in a bank or investing in share market or in another business?

The financial viability exercise starts with estimating investment and operating costs and, therefore, capital requirements (including working capital) to be funded through equity and debt.

Projected financial statements like Balance Sheet, Cash Flow and Profit& Loss Statements provide the data to generate such ratios as: Break-even Analysis, Payback Period, Return on Equity/Investment, Debt Service Coverage Ratio and Internal Rate of Return.

RISK/REWARD PROFILE AND SENSITIVITY ANALYSIS

What are the main sources of risks for the new venture? Such risks include customer/market risk, technology risk, regulatory risk and broad economic or social risk. Which of these risks can you control? Which are outside your control? Can your business model be adjusted to accommodate such risks?

Two or three scenarios of possible outcomes of the new venture are to be constructed. The financial performance of the venture under each of these scenarios should be described in relation to the core assumptions that underlie each scenario.

The key results of a 'what if' analysis based on 'best' and 'worst' case situations may be presented. What would be the financial outcome (or additional funding requirements) if sales volumes and prices are both 90% of targets but direct and overhead costs are each 110% of what were estimated?

9.4 PRUDENT FINANCIAL PLANNING

"We are frugal with capital because we know that entrepreneurship is the art of staying alive long enough to get lucky."

—**Manish Sabharwal,** Co-Founder, TeamLease

You will be better off being realistic than fatalistic or optimistic. Plan to follow conservative financial management practices to present the enterprise in its financial best light to attract bank credit lines and outside financing.

Cash flow projections are based on a set of assumptions. If any of the assumptions does not hold up, the cash required will be much more than what is provided for.

Over-capitalization need not necessarily kill an enterprise; undercapitalization does. Low initial capital base means raising capital the second or the third time for the new project. This process can be more difficult than raising the full amount needed at the beginning.

It is best to keep most costs variable, postponing inessential investments. Keep the "burn rate", especially during the initial phase, as low as possible. Cash disbursements are to be ruthlessly prioritized to avoid depletion of cash reserves – high priority payroll and essential vendor payments. Disbursements should be timed to coincide with cash inflows.

   a) **Managing Accounts Receivable**: Do monthly ageing exercises to track how much of your money is tied up in credit given to customers and trade to get a sense of slow payment problems, if any; shorten the ' payment due' period.

b) **Managing Accounts Payable**: Whom to pay, when? Paying too early can deplete cash; paying too late can deny the benefit of discounts for prompt payment besides creating bad image.

A wide range of appropriate ratios is to be calculated to assess the quality of financial management.

9.5 MINDING CASH FLOW

Cash flow is your business's lifeblood. Cash flow statement indicates whether you are spending more than what you are earning. Cash gives you freedom; financial resilience helps you ride out the inevitable ups and downs while building the business.

Capital investment is a negative cash flow. The amount of time required to fully recover the original capital investment through positive cash flows is the payback time. Keeping the payback time as short as possible will help Startups grow fast.

The saying "revenue is vanity, cash flow is sanity, but cash is king" highlights why growing revenue from sales (which may include credit sale of goods) is fine but positive cash flow (the business is receiving more money than it is spending) is vital to the health of a business.

9.6 INSTITUTIONAL FUNDING

Small Industries Development Bank of India (SIDBI) provides both direct assistance as well as indirect assistance by refinancing the assistance given by the State-level institutions. The range of direct assistance includes:

1. Term loans and Working Capital loans for new units as well as expansion/diversification/modernization/technology upgrading /quality certification etc. for existing businesses.

2. Existing enterprises are also offered assistance under the following schemes:

    a) Receivables Financing Scheme, to realize their sales proceeds quickly.

    b) Post-shipment Credit in foreign currency at competitive rates of interest.

c) Post-shipment Rupee Credit.

d) Risk Capital Fund in the form of equity/equity-like investments.

3. In August 2015, SIDBI launched two funds with a total corpus of Rs. 120 billion – Indian Aspiration Fund (IAF) and SIDBI Make in India Loan for Enterprises (SMILE). IAF is expected to catalyze tens of thousands of Startups and MSMEs by providing equity investment. SMILE scheme is to provide soft-loans in the nature of quasi-equity and term loans on soft-terms to MSMEs (See details at www.sidbi.com).

Micro Units Development and Refinance Agency Ltd. (MUDRA Bank) launched in 2015, to meet the credit needs of small enterprises whose requirements do not exceed Rs.1 million per enterprise. Such units include small retailers/shop keepers, women enterprises and manufacturing and service enterprises. MUDRA will provide refinance assistance to commercial banks, NBFCs, RRBs, Cooperative Banks and MFIs that offer financial assistance to the small enterprises (See details of the financial and non-financial assistance of the bank at www.mudra.org.in).

Newly launched **Bandhan Bank**, the first micro finance agency transformed into a scheduled commercial bank, will meet the requirements of the unbanked population in the unorganized sector. The loan to micro/small enterprises including shop keepers and hawkers, mostly in the East and North East regions, will range from Rs. 50,000 to Rs. 500,000. According to the Ministry of Finance, Govt. of India, such micro/small enterprises annually generate 110–120 million jobs.

Ministry of Science and Technology, Govt. of India, under its Technopreneur Promotion Programme provides financial and technical support for translating new ideas into marketable products.

National Entrepreneurship Network, India offers the following comments on financing Startup enterprises in the country: As per a survey, 70% of the people interviewed cited personal savings as the primary source of funding for starting their entrepreneurial ventures, followed by loans from family and friends (27%) and bank loans and angel investors (4%).

Government entities across the world at the National, State and even Municipal levels offer financial assistance of varying kinds to SMEs. Singapore government funding initiatives to support SMEs include:

Start-up Enterprise Development Scheme, Business Angels Scheme, Growth Financing Programme, Micro-Loan Programme, Local Enterprise Finance Scheme, Loan Insurance Scheme, Export Coverage Scheme, Internationalization Finance Scheme and Venture Capital/Private Equity Support.

For SMEs, the issue is not necessarily identifying a variety of sources of funds. **The issue is how best to access such funds under the best terms and use them wisely.**

9.7 ANGEL INVESTORS AND VENTURE CAPITALISTS

In developed economies, Angel Funds and Venture Capitalist (VC) Funds are two major sources of funding for Startups.

Business Angels are private individuals who provide Seed funding, relatively small amounts based on an idea. They invest their own wealth in enterprises on the assumption that they will get higher returns when the ventures get "discovered" at some point in time by buyers who will pay hefty premium.

VC funds (private equity) are provided by professionals (who manage such funds on behalf of investors in such funds) who invest alongside the promoters in young enterprises having the potential for growth. Venture Capitalists help build the team, get customers, secure follow-on rounds of funding and add value to the venture through active participation. When the valuation is right, they exit with their investments having grown several times the original value.

VC funds may be invested in all stages of an entrepreneurial firm's development, from Seed through expansion stages; however, mostly they invest in the post-Seed stage.

1. **Seed stage**: The development phase prior to establishing commercial operations when founders conduct research, determine product features and explore market potential.
2. **Startup stage**: The firm is in the process of establishing the facilities and bringing the product to the market. This stage generally requires a lot of capital for acquiring fixed assets and meeting operational expenses without any revenue.
3. **Expansion stage**: Capital is required to finance growth.

VC Funds look for answers to such questions as:

1. What is unique about the product/project and how is the product differentiated from competition? Does the enterprise have the potential to become a leader in the chosen market?
2. How does or how will the company attain profitability?
3. How will the funds be utilized?
4. Is the management capable of implementing the project as planned? Does the team have strong exposure to the industry or market it is addressing?
5. What is the exit strategy for the investors?

(For a list of active VC/Angel Funds in India, visit nenonline.org/resource)

9.8 BOOTSTRAPPING

A survival principle for Startups, Bootstrapping is using own money (savings, borrowings against asset such as home) to start the business with minimal infusion of outside funds. Growth is funded through sales. Bootstrapping process has, of course, obvious limits.

Explore the ways to reduce capital requirement:

a) Spend less: Be totally aware of where every Rupee goes and refuse to spend on anything not strictly relevant.
b) Borrow or rent or lease assets instead of buying them.
c) Start with used office furniture or even second-hand machinery instead of buying new.
d) Take advantage of other firms' unused capacity.
e) Ask your vendors for more generous payment terms.
f) Convince customers to pay in advance.
g) Take on merchandise on a consignment basis rather than purchase it.
h) Living off your spouse's salary while starting the business.

i) Learn to barter: Offer proof reading service in exchange for an advertisement for your business in a publication!

j) Going as long as possible without paying yourself.

With creativity, commitment and resilience, an entrepreneur can turn even a small investment into an impressive business.

Today, bootstrapping entrepreneurs have the benefit of technological tools which were not available some years ago. For instance, professional-looking websites and automated phone-answering systems can speed sales and make a Startup look more impressive and professional to prospective customers. Thanks to the proliferation of the Internet and the availability of once-costly technology, Startup costs have plummeted in the recent past. Today, it is so much easier to reach mass markets and test your ideas.

9.9 ILLUSTRATIVE LIST OF FINANCIAL AND NON-FINANCIAL ASSISTANCE

I. SMALL ENTERPRISE ASSISTANCE FUND (SEAF)

Financial support from SEAF

Across its international network of offices, SEAF's investment team seeks to provide promising small and medium enterprises (SMEs) with customized financial products adapted to the unique economic, cultural, and regulatory requirements of each of the markets. The investments take the form of equity, mezzanine, and term credit.

1. **Equity**: SEAF will invest through common or preferred stock to take an equity ownership position in portfolio companies. It will typically take minority positions with significant governance and information rights, but may elect to take majority positions for certain opportunities.

    a) Structure: Common or preferred stock

    b) Investment amount: Generally $500,000 to $3,000,000

2. **Mezzanine**: SEAF's mezzanine investments are generally subordinated loans that combine current interest payments with a participation in revenue, earnings growth or enterprise value.

a) Structure: 5+ year term, Flexible Amortization

b) Investment amount: Generally $200,000 to $3,000,000

c) Equity-type participation: Revenue participation, variable or payment in-kind interest, conversion options, warrants

3. **Term Credit:** SEAF also provides lines of credit, working capital loans, and trade financing for certain companies.

a) Structure: Medium to long term, flexible amortization

b) Investment amount: Generally $200,000 to $3, 000,000

Business assistance from SEAF

Center for Entrepreneurship and Executive Development (www.ceed-global.org), under SEAF, provides entrepreneurs business know-how through its accelerator programs and also connects participants to mentors and to a community of entrepreneurs that can help take their small business to the next level. The holistic combination of market connections, community engagement, capacity building, and access to capital is very helpful.

II. SME FINANCE FACILITATION CENTER (mycii.in)

An initiative of the Confederation of the Indian Industry (CII), this knowledge portal supported by CII offices across the country provides a range of assistance to those SMEs seeking financial assistance. The services include updates on the latest schemes of the Central and State governments and financial institutions. Advisory is provided on preparing the documents required by lending institutions.

III. SME TOOLKIT (www.india.smetoolkit.org)

The SME Toolkit is a joint project between ICICI Bank and IFC, a member of the World Bank Group. The SME Toolkit website is an online resource centre providing comprehensive and easy to use information on a variety of topics like Business Planning, Accounting, HR, International Business, Legal, Insurance, Taxation, Marketing Operations, Technology and Tenders.

IV. MSME SCHEMES (http://www.msme.gov.in/)

The Ministry of MSME, Govt. of India provides details of the several services and support programmes under the different schemes for MSMEs.

Select schemes for building competitiveness among MSMEs, are listed below:

1. **Credit Guarantee for MSMEs**: To catalyze flow of bank credit to first generation entrepreneurs for setting up their enterprises/existing ones for scaling up without hassles of secondary collateral/third party guarantees.

   a) The credit facilities covered under the scheme are both term loans and/or working capital facility up to Rs. 10 million.

   b) The guarantee cover provided up to 75% of the credit facility with a maximum of Rs. 5 million 85% for loans up to Rs. 0.5 million provided to Micro enterprises.

   c) With a uniform guarantee at 50% for the entire amount if the credit exposure is above Rs. 5 million and up to Rs. 10 million.

2. **Credit Linked Capital Subsidy Scheme:** To facilitate technology up-gradation of Micro and Small enterprises by providing 15% capital subsidy (limited to a maximum of Rs. 1.5 million) for purchase of plant and machinery.

3. **Quality Up-gradation/Environment Management for Small Scale Sector through Incentive for ISO 9000/ISO 14001/HACCP Certification:** Reimbursement of charges for acquiring the above certifications to the extent to 75% of the expenditure subject to a maximum of Rs. 75,000 in each case.

4. **Market Development Assistance:** To promote participation by manufacturing Small and Micro Enterprises in International Trade Fairs/Exhibitions, financial assistance on Bar Code to enhance the competitiveness of MSMEs.

5. **Cluster Development Programme:** Covering cost of diagnostic study, setting up of Common Facility Centres (CFCs) and Infrastructure Development, mostly funded by the Government of India.

6. **National Manufacturing Competitiveness Programme**
    a) Incubator scheme limited to Rs. 6.25 million for 10 units.
    b) Lean Manufacturing covering such LM techniques as SS System, Standard Operating Procedures, Just in Time, KANBAN System, Cellular Layout and Kazan Blitz or Rapid Improvement Process.
    c) Intellectual Property Rights
    d) Quality Management Standards and Quality Technology Tools
    e) Adopting IT Tools and Applications
    f) Technology and Quality Up-gradation Support
    g) Design Clinic

V. TECHNOLOGY ACQUISITION AND DEVELOPMENT FUND
(http://www.dipp.gov.in/English/default.aspx)

The various schemes of TADF include:

1. **Direct Technology Acquisition**: Reimbursement of 50% of technology transfer fee or Rs. 2 million, whichever is lower.
2. **In-direct Technology Acquisition**: Subsidy of 50% of the mutually agreed value or Rs 2 million, whichever is lower.
3. **Subsidy for Manufacturing Equipment/Technology**: Subsidy of up to 10% of capital expenditure incurred on new Plant & Machinery subject a maximum of Rs 5 million.
4. **Incentive Scheme for Green Manufacturing**: The scheme facilitates resource conservation activities in industries located in NIMZ through the introduction of incentive/subsidy schemes for energy/environmental/water audits, construction of green buildings, implementation of waste treatment Facilities and implementation of renewable energy projects.

VI. CROWDFUNDING
(An innovative financing option originated in the USA)

Equity funding through online platforms has become the newest channel for Startup companies to raise capital. Crowdfunding Platforms like Ketto, LetsVenture, Equity Crest and GREX mobilize funds from investors looking for good returns. Startups with high growth potential are chosen for funding. Each deal could range between, say, Rs.2.5 million to Rs.50 million.

Equity Crowdfunding is possible even before a Startup is commissioned. However, the promoter has to clearly establish the potential of the product and the financial viability of the business before investors are invited to participate in the funding. A thorough due diligence is undertaken by the professionals of these platforms to establish the competence of the promoter and the prospects of the business.

VII. SBI INCUBE

State Bank of India InCube branch is a specialized branch to understand and address the banking needs of Startups. The branch will provide the most appropriate solutions in banking transactions and investments on a technology platform. The services include advisory on:

a) Comprehensive, competitively priced financial products and services.

b) Integrated online and mobile banking solutions to save the time and money of promoters.

c) Investments, taxation and foreign exchange transactions that help optimize liquidity, capital preservation and return.

SBI InCube is not planning to provide loans to Startups in the initial phase.

VIII. SELF-EMPLOYMENT AND TALENT UTILIZATION PROGRAMME

Government of India launched in December 2015 the Self-Employment and Talent Utilization (SETU) programme aimed at comprehensive support for Startups and self-employment. The goal of the programme is to foster entrepreneurship and innovation at the grass-roots level by providing fiscal incentives, market linkages, legal support and creation of grass-roots technology innovation hubs.

IX. STARTUP-INDIA ACTION PLAN

Govt. of India announced on Jan 16, 2016 a comprehensive Action Plan to create the right eco-system for nurturing innovative Startups, which will generate large-scale employment opportunities and drive sustainable economic growth. The steps envisaged include:

a) Easing the regulatory burden through a compliance regime based on self-certification

b) Rolling-out of Mobile App and Portal to serve as the single platform for Startups for interacting with government and regulatory institutions. This would enable the registration of Startups within a day.

c) 3-year Income Tax holiday

d) Capital Gain Tax exempted for Venture Capital investments

e) Providing funding support through a Fund of Funds with a corpus of Rs. 25 billion annually over 4 years to finance Startups

f) Allocation of Rs. 5 billion for SC/ST and women entrepreneurs

g) Legal support and fast tracking of Patent creation process; Patent fee reduced by 80%. A special patent regime with a 10% rate of tax on income from worldwide exploitation of patents developed and registered in India was announced in the 2016–17 budget of Government of India.

h) A Startup India hub to be created as a single point of contact to enable knowledge creation and access to funding.

i) Relaxed norms of public procurement for Startups

j) Faster exit for Startups under hostile business conditions

k) Credit guarantee fund for Startups to help the flow of debt fund from banking system by providing guarantee against risks.

l) Entrepreneurship learning through Massive Open Online Courses to provide access to educational resources across the country.

10
How Best to Manage Operations

Doing Things Right, Doing the Right Things

10.1 DEFINING OPERATIONS MANAGEMENT

Operations Management (OM) is concerned with the principles of: General Management; Manufacturing and Production Systems; Plant Management; Equipment Maintenance Management; Production Control; Supervision of Professionals and Workers; Strategic Manufacturing Policy; Systems Analysis; Productivity; Cost Control; Materials Planning; Management of Money.

The Association for Operations Management defines OM as: *"... the effective planning, scheduling, use and control of a manufacturing or service organization through the study of concepts from design engineering, industrial engineering, management information systems, quality management, production management, inventory management, accounting and other functions as they affect the organization."*

OM is all about an enterprise finding the best way to do what they do. OM is focused on:

a) Reducing product lead-times.
b) Efficient and effective operation: Using the least amount of resources, in the fewest steps.
c) Superior product quality and reliability.
d) Alignment with the customer needs and wants, conforming to pre-defined specifications.
e) Competitive pricing while delivering value.

The bottom line is that the intrinsic value and income-generating potential of an asset can be maximized only if it is taken full advantage of and managed well.

Performance metrics: You should regularly be asking such questions as:

1. What am I doing?
2. How well am I doing it?
3. How do I know how well am I doing?
4. Am I using the right benchmarks/standards to determine how well am I doing it?
5. Am I placing the interests of my customers at the heart of everything I do?
6. How can I demonstrate to others how well am I doing it?

A wide range of operating ratios are used to measure an enterprise's operating efficiency and effectiveness by relating various income and expense figures from the Profit and Loss Statement to each other and to Balance Sheet figures.

Operating Ratio – [(cost of goods sold + operating expenses)/net sales] x 100 – shows the operating efficiency of the business. Lower Operating Ratio means higher operating profit and vice versa. An Operating Ratio ranging from 75% to 80% is generally treated as standard for manufacturing firms.

The pre-requisites for organizational efficiency include:

a) Appropriate organizational structure and internal processes: Rigid, hierarchical structures cause inefficiency essentially by the duplication of efforts
b) Employee morale
c) Entire supply chain – suppliers, distributors and consumers – being under control. Unreliable supplies disrupt production.
d) Quality mindset
e) Cycle time, defect rate etc. to be closely monitored, measured and benchmarked against best-in-class practices.
f) Statutory and policy compliance: Knowingly or unknowingly flouting any statutory rule causes complications.

10.2 SEEKING OPERATIONAL EXCELLENCE

In a fiercely competitive environment, the product price has to be competitive; cost reduction, through whatever means available including innovative technology is, therefore, critical for survival.

Operational excellence is about delivering an acceptable product at the lowest total cost with the least inconvenience to customers by focusing on cost management and operational effectiveness. It is determined by the effective use of available resources like people, time, money, materials, facilities and knowledge. Productivity of an enterprise is improved by increasing the output without increasing the inputs or increasing the inputs less proportionately than the increase in output by streamlining the underlying processes to eliminate unnecessary steps and adding capabilities to the underlying processes that get higher ratio of output to input.

Companies seeking operational excellence also keep customer satisfaction as a vital goal. All processes are fine-tuned to ensure that customer needs are met fully by delivering quality products at competitive price.

10.3 PROCESS REENGINEERING

"An organization is only as effective as its processes."

Process Reengineering has been a buzzword gaining popularity in the recent past. It is, in fact, a concept applicable to all businesses regardless of size or type. It:

a) Involves redesigning or reinventing how an enterprise performs its daily work.

b) Makes an enterprise more flexible, responsive, efficient and effective for their customers, employees and other stakeholders.

c) Improves measures of performance: Cost, quality, service and speed.

Process Reengineering could begin with Business Process Mapping:

a) Defining what a business entity does.

b) Understanding the existing processes.

c) Simplifying the processes by eliminating non-value added activities.

d) Determining who does what.

e) Specifying to what standard a process should be completed.

f) Figuring out how the success of a business process can be determined.

10.4 EFFICIENCY VS. EFFECTIVENESS: PERILS OF PURSUING PERFECTION

Being efficient means doing things quickly and properly: **Doing things right**. Being effective means knowing what your priorities are and **doing the right things at the right time**.

You face a Catch-22 situation here:

1. Management of efficiency aims at minimizing the resources and time needed to complete a process. Being efficient means being consistent, being consistent means being wedded to rules, processes and systems. Being consistent, therefore, means being a victim of staleness brought on by repetition and boredom both for customers as well as for those who work in an enterprise whereas creativity and motivation are now being valued as competitive advantages.

2. Mindless pursuit of efficiency arguably can lead to an unhappy situation. Your internal operation may be very efficient; but then, you could well be trying to sell the wrong product. To quote Ron Baker, "The buggy whip manufacturers were highly efficient the day before they went out of business." Automobiles hit the scene! Had the strategists of the industry been effective, they would have anticipated the impending threats and looked for other options.

3. Effectiveness means being nimble-footed, adapting quickly, reinventing oneself through innovation arising from a complete understanding of what customers want. Essentially, it means being inconsistent and, therefore, somewhat inefficient.

4. Effective businesses concentrate on the effectiveness of their products and solutions to meet customer requirements and to beat competitive pressures. Such an approach alone can ensure success over the long run.

In the final reckoning, it is not an either/or option. Even the most effective enterprise has to be efficient to survive. Once again, it is yet another tight-rope-walk for the entrepreneur.

11
Rules of Success Recommended by Those Who Succeeded

11.1 WELVE RULES OF SUCCESS (STEVE JOBS, APPLE INC.)

1. *Do what you love to do*
2. *Be different*
3. *Do your best*
4. *Make SWOT analysis*
5. *Be entrepreneurial*
6. *Start small, think big*
7. *Strive to become a market leader*
8. *Focus on the outcome*
9. *Ask for feedback*
10. *Innovate*
11. *Learn from failures*
12. *Learn continually*

11.2 SEVEN-POINT PROGRAMME (JACK WELCH, FORMER CEO OF GE)

1. *Develop a vision for the business*
2. *Change the culture to achieve the vision*
3. *Flatten the organization*
4. *Eliminate bureaucracy*
5. *Empower individuals*

6. Raise quality and efficiency
7. Eliminate boundaries

11.3 "TEN COMMANDMENTS" FOR THE BEGINNING ENTREPRENEUR (PROF. LIORA KATZENSTEIN, PRESIDENT, ISEMI)

1. Raise capital when you don't need it: a typical entrepreneur is always in a constant race in search of financing sources. The right time to look for new finance is at the beginning of each step, while there are still some cash reserves.
2. Focus on a well-defined limited business field/niche: entrepreneurs often make the mistake of trying to cover too many subjects at the same time.
3. Listen to expert advice and don't hesitate to pay for professional services: entrepreneurs tend to think they "know it all".
4. Choose a team of professionals and don't compromise on the quality of manpower:
5. Don't "argue" with the market: many entrepreneurs think they know better what the market's demands are.
6. Develop a Strategic business vision as early as possible and learn from your own mistakes
7. Enlist the support of your family and friends.
8. Define correctly the comparative advantage of your product from the user's standpoint.
9. Stay in touch and learn from other entrepreneurs – network.
10. Learn about the "life cycles" of the entrepreneur and the business: When the business succeeds leave the business and concentrate on what he is really good at it - starting other new businesses.

11.4 FIVE SECRETS (F.W. SMITH, CHAIRMAN, FEDEX CORPORATION)

1. Have a compelling business idea; one that is differentiated and sustainable. You must be the first or the fastest or the most convenient or must deliver more value for money

2. *You must be a zealot having unlimited enthusiasm to press on till you succeed*
3. *Have a conservative business plan; thorough, hard data to support the assumptions made*
4. *Work effectively with others; persuading, motivating and inspiring the team*
5. *Change and grow as your business grows*

11.5 TEN RULES FOR SMALL BUSINESS SUCCESS (ISABEL M. ISIDRO)

1. *Find a niche*
2. *Be small, yet think big: Compete with big players by leveraging the advantages of flexibility, ability to respond quickly, able to provide a more personalized service.*
3. *Differentiate your product*
4. *First impression counts: strive for accuracy and quality the first time around.*
5. *Good reputation: your business hinges on its reputation.*
6. *Constant improvement*
7. *Listen to your customers*
8. *Plan for success*
9. *Be innovative*
10. *Work smart*

12
1 To 1 Billion: Seven Exponential Entrepreneurial Stories*

The identified 7 entrepreneurs and the enterprises they built could well be ranked among the most transformational stories of our times. They demonstrate that one idea– nurtured by an innovative entrepreneur in a supportive ecosystem – can create a billion devices, generate a billion dollars or touch a billion people. The chosen artifacts exemplify the 7 stories.

HP Model 200 Oscillator(1939)

This product built by Stanford University graduates, Bill Hewlett and Dave Packard, was at the heart of their new company, Hewlett-Packard, founded in 1939. Today it comprises two companies with a combined worth of $52 billion. HP made unmatched contribution to help shape Silicon Valley and to management practice in general.

Fairchild Notebooks (1967)

One set of engineering notebooks, including those by Gordon Moore and Jay Last, co-founders of Fairchild, revealed the roots of today's $360 billion semiconductor industry which helped found Silicon Valley.

Micro-Soft Altair Basic (1975)

A BASIC interpreter for the Altair 8800 microcomputer written by Bill Gates and Paul Allen led to the creation of the software company

---

* Adapted from an online article by Marguerite Gong Hancock Exponential Centre, Computer History Museum, Silicon Valley.

they co-found, Micro-Soft. Microsoft Office, one of the products of the company, used by 1.2 billion people around the world.

Apple Offering Memo (1978)

One risky business plan, by co-founders Steve Jobs and Steve Wozniak laid the foundation for Apple. Its brand now tops the rank of most valuable world brands. As of July 2016, Apple is the most valuable company on NASDAQ with a market capitalization of over $580 billion; it also celebrated the sale of the billionth iPhone.

Cisco AGS Router (1986)

One innovation, Cisco's AGS Router launched in 1986 by Cisco co-founders, Sandy Lerner and Len Bosak, established Cisco as a leading supplier of network infrastructure equipment, with around 3.4 billion Internet users per year.

Facebook Motherboard (2011)

One motherboard created for the Open Computer Service project, founded by Facebook in 2011, disrupted the $141 billion data converter computer hardware market and also enabled Facebook, led by Mark Zuckerberg, to provide services by June 2016 to an average of more than 1.3 billion daily active users.

Google Bicycle (2011)

One invention in online advertising, Google Adwords, revolutionized the business model for online search. Founded by Larry Page and Sergey Brin, Google maintains a fleet of colourful bikes for employees. This innovation fuelled the development of Google, which now powers 3.5 billion searches per day to access the world's information.

13

Entrepreneurship: The Widely Debated But Barely Understood Concept

"... Entrepreneurship, a word in search of a meaning"

The hypothesis, which should essentially be uncontested, that entrepreneurship originates overwhelmingly from the entrepreneurial instincts of individuals opens a window to the elusive nature of the phenomenon; after all, instinct is innate impulsion, intuition and acting without conscious intervention.

Let us now introduce a somewhat more concrete hypothesis (than the one we started with) to get a sense of the conceptual conundrums we can drift into. **The key to the success of an enterprise is getting four vital factors to be in balance: Sales/profit margin/quality of the product/operational efficiency**. The more you look at this proposition, the more you are aware of its complexity.

How does an enterprise **increase sales revenue**?

a) By selling more at the same price.

b) By selling the same quantity at higher price or selling part of the quantity at the same price and the rest of the quantity at higher prices to those customer groups which are not price-sensitive so that the average price realization is higher.

c) By diversifying into new product lines yielding higher sales revenue. But the existing facility may not accommodate diversification; you have, therefore, to install new sets of equipment etc. The additional investment (for diversification or expansion) can, in the short-run, contract the profit margin. An enterprise can expand sales beyond a point only by expanding installed capacity. Installing additional capacity involves additional investments as well as hiring more people. The additional investments have to be funded through additional loans (and equity) which would imply provisions for interest as well as for depreciation on the fixed capital added. If the unit cost of production has to be maintained, additional sales need to be large enough to cover the cost of additional investments - essentially depreciation and interest.

How does an enterprise **improve the profit margin**?

1. By selling more at the same price or selling the same quantity at higher prices. When you sell more (and, therefore, have to produce more) even without raising the price you tend to get the benefit of scale because:

    a) Your unit cost of production comes down because your unit fixed cost comes down.

    b) You order more inputs from your suppliers who may give you a discount, thereby reducing the unit cost of input.

2. By improving operational efficiency

    How does an entrepreneur **raise the price, without losing market share (in value terms)**?

    a) By improving the quality/functionality of the product or by giving better services to customers than competition or taking advantage of product shortage (Not particularly a customer-friendly act!).

    b) By redesigning the product to target the high-end market segment thereby capturing higher price per unit.

How does one **define quality of a product**? Is it in terms of a product's functionality/durability? Could it be that part of it is a perception of the customer?

How does an enterprise **improve the quality of the product**?

By better process technology, higher commitment to a zero-defect operational philosophy, keener involvement of workers, stronger controls on inputs etc.

How does one determine operational efficiency of a given company? What parameters to be used? Normally, the performance of one company is benchmarked against the best of the league; the issue is the choice of parameters. In any case, can two companies be at all compared? Using industry averages is an option.

How does an enterprise **improve the operational efficiency**? : The possibilities include incorporating better process technology; installing state-of-the-art plant & machinery; improving the plant layout; enhancing the productivity of workers by giving them training and performance-driven rewards; pursuing zero-waste (materials as well as efforts) initiatives; better control of purchase of inputs; and installing processes and equipment for saving utilities.

How does one **define the balance**? Is there a set of metrics that explains the phenomenon? Can there at all be a balancing act?

To be successful, an enterprise should keep increasing the sales, improving the profit margins, ensuring quality of the product and enhancing operational efficiency. The balance we are talking about is not necessarily to be achieved every year or at a pre-determined date or time. It should be looked at as a goal to aspire to and work towards. It is not as if a company achieves a balance in whatever fashion you define it and then can relax. In fact, there is nothing like a 'permanent' balance. Most enterprises may be in an unending struggle chasing an unattainable balance.

a) For instance, an enterprise raises the price. Immediately, the profit margin may go up. But it can adversely affect its sales when some of the customers will shift to cheaper alternatives; capacity utilization will fall and unit cost of production could go up and eventually profit margins will be hit.

b) When sales fall, an enterprise may reduce the price to retain its market share. The fall in price could upset the profit margin unless the operational efficiency is simultaneously improved.

May be, we should argue that most everything relating to an enterprise is inter-related. You can't isolate any one parameter and 'manipulate' it without causing a range of consequences, some good and some bad.

No question in the field of entrepreneurship seems to yield a credible answer; no answer seems valid for long. The intense debate on most of the fundamental aspects relating to entrepreneur and entrepreneurship is far from resolved. This problem stalks management science in general. Even widely trusted and practiced principles of management periodically get demolished in light of new evidence or merely by redefining or reinterpreting the basic assumptions.

"Nine-tenths of the approximately 100 branded management ideas I've studied lost their popularity within a decade or so" - Julian Birkinshaw, faculty at the London Business School

David Gumpert, a popular writer on small businesses wrote two books on Business Plan: How to Really Create a Successful Business Plan and Burn Your Business Plan!!

Some segments of the subject of business management seem to reflect the essence of the metaphor, searching in a dark room for a black cat that isn't there. The most intriguing, however, is **entrepreneurship, one of the most observed or debated and yet the least understood phenomena in the realm of business management.**

PART III
Impact of Social & Economic Environment on Entrepreneurship Development

Nurturing entrepreneurship is helping individuals "*take a chance on a dream – taking an idea that starts around kitchen table or in a garage and turning it into a new business, and even new industries, that can change the world*" – Barack Obama, President of the United States of America.

14
Impact of the Environment on Entrepreneurship Development

14.1 ENABLING ECOSYSTEM TO HARNESS ENTREPRENEURIAL INSTINCTS

Entrepreneurship is reckoned to be an omnipresent aspect of human behaviour. But its flowering depends upon an enabling environment which must nurture and sustain entrepreneurship ecosystems.

Entrepreneurship is a critical driver of innovation and economic growth. Therefore, fostering entrepreneurship is an important part of the growth strategies of many local and national governments around the world. Governments assist in the development of entrepreneurial ecosystem which includes entrepreneurs, venture capitalists and other funding agencies, government entities, universities, mentors, service providers, entrepreneurs' associations and large companies.

The challenge is to get more people to consider self-employment and business creation:

a) As job creators and not job seekers, to quote a popular slogan
b) As a viable and attractive option, a demanding but rewarding and achievable goal.

THE COMPELLING NEED FOR AN ENABLING ECOSYSTEM

"... A range of environmental conditions affect three main components of entrepreneurship: attitudes, activity and aspirations and that this dynamic mix produces new economic and socially valuable activity, generating jobs and wealth."

—**Global Entrepreneurship Monitor (GEM)
2009 Executive Report**

"... No matter how fertile the seeds of entrepreneurship, they wither without the proper economic soil. In order for entrepreneurship to germinate, take root and yield the fruits of economic progress, it has to be nourished by the right mixture of freedom and accountability, a mixture that can only be provided by a free market economy."

—Dwight Lee, The Economist

"Entrepreneurship thrives in an ecosystem in which multiple stakeholders play a role in facilitating entrepreneurship. Policy-makers at the international, national, regional and local levels all have important roles to play in setting the appropriate legal and fiscal framework to encourage entrepreneurship and to fill market gaps as necessary."

—Global Ventures Partners, Business Advisory firm

Social and economic environment and political institutions that govern the market process (political stability, rule of law and voice in government affairs) impact strongly on individual's willingness to take risks associated with investing, starting and managing new businesses. The ecosystem must encourage enterprises to innovate, develop skills and human resources and enhance productivity to remain competitive in national and international markets.

The components of the enabling ecosystem in which entrepreneurship flourishes include:

a) Simplified procedures for starting or expanding or closing an enterprise.

b) Low administrative burdens and compliance costs.

c) Simplified taxes and duties.

d) Helpful labour laws – flexible employment contracts, ease of retrenchment under hostile business conditions.

e) Availability of different kinds of finance and financial incentives.

f) Vibrant education system generating quality human capital.

g) Robust infrastructure facilities.

h) Consultancy and training.

i) Tolerance to company failures without any stigma; benign bankruptcy regulations.

j) Positive social and cultural attitudes towards entrepreneurship.

Entrepreneurship flourishes in communities where:

a) Resources are mobile.

b) Successful members of the community invest excess capital in projects of other community members. Success of other community members is celebrated and not derided.

Many World Bank studies show that entrepreneurship activities and the creation of formal enterprises are hampered, if the initial processes of getting a new enterprise incorporated are complicated, time-consuming and costly. Simpler Startup processes are associated with higher rates of formal entrepreneurship, lesser development of 'shadow economies' (informal entities), increased tax revenue and decreased corruption.

Even the most enthusiastic entrepreneur can be deterred from pursuing new ventures if opportunity costs (forgone salary etc.) and Startup costs outweigh the potential benefits.

Daniel J. Isenberg (Professor of Entrepreneurship Practice at Babson College, USA) observes, *"...There is no exact formula for creating an entrepreneurial economy; there are only practical, if imperfect, road maps... The entrepreneurial ecosystem consists of a set of individual elements - such as leadership, culture, capital markets and open-minded customers – that combine in complex ways."* He suggests a set of prescriptions for creating an entrepreneurship ecosystem:

a) Shape the ecosystem around the local conditions.

b) Engage the private sector from the start.

c) Favor the high potential enterprises: Don't spread the limited resources among too many entities.

d) Reform legal, bureaucratic and regulatory framework.

On the basis of extensive studies of international experiences, OECD observes that entrepreneurs and entrepreneurship are created by a combination of 3 factors: Opportunities, people with entrepreneurial capabilities and resources. The surrounding regulatory framework, market conditions or opportunities and culture, in turn, impact these determinants.

1. Market conditions and opportunities reflect competition in the market, access to foreign markets, procurement regulation and so on.

2. Availability of people with entrepreneurial capabilities is a function of business and entrepreneurship education, training and experience of entrepreneurs, entrepreneurship infrastructure, immigration etc.
3. Resources: Access to capital (debt financing, venture capital and other types of equity), R&D and technology, which yield new inventions, university-industry interfaces, patent systems, technology diffusion etc.
4. Regulatory framework: Administrative burdens for entry and growth; regulations on bankruptcy, health, environment, safety issues and labour market; taxation etc.
5. Culture: Entrepreneurial culture of a society influences an entrepreneur's behaviour and attitudes; some societies are positively inclined to entrepreneurs and their success and do everything possible to mitigate such risks as those faced by venture creators.

14.2 GLOBAL ENTREPRENEURSHIP MONITOR (GEM) REPORTS

Global Entrepreneurship Research Association prepares GEM reports and research papers under the leadership of Babson College, USA and London Business School. GEM is an annual assessment of entrepreneurial activity, aspirations and attitudes of individuals across a range of countries. GEM explores the role of entrepreneurship in national economic growth, unveiling detailed national features and characteristics associated with entrepreneurial activity.

Entrepreneurial Framework Conditions as stipulated by GEM are:

1. Financial Support
2. Government Policies
3. Government Programmes
4. Entrepreneurship Education and Training
5. R&D Transfer
6. Commercial and Legal Infrastructure

7. Entry Regulation
8. Access to Physical Infrastructure
9. Cultural, Social Norms

Countries with poor business environments – costly regulations, bureaucracy, poor credit and banking system – tend to have a large 'shadow' sector whose commercial activities are conducted outside the regulatory environment – hiring casual labour (without the benefits that those formally employed enjoy), tax evasion etc. In such environments, those with formal jobs account for only less than 10% of the total workforce.

14.3 OPTIMIZING THE REGULATORY ENVIRONMENT (UNCTAD)

UNCTAD prescribes the following steps to ease the process of dealing with the regulatory environment for Startups:

1. **Examine regulatory requirements for Startups**
   a) Benchmark time and cost of starting a business
   b) Benchmark sector and region-specific regulations
   c) Set up public-private dialogue on regulatory costs and benefits
   d) Balance regulation and standards with sustainable development objectives.

2. **Minimize regulatory hurdles for business Startups where appropriate**
   a) Review and, where appropriate, reduce regulatory requirements (e.g. licenses, procedures, administrative fees)
   b) Introduce transparent information and fast-track mechanisms and one-stop-shops to bundle procedures
   c) Enhance ICT-based procedures for business registration and reporting. (There is a strong case for pursuing e-government initiatives to spur entrepreneurship. In countries with electronic registration, starting a business takes less time, requires fewer procedures and costs less.)

3. **Build entrepreneurs' confidence in the regulatory environment**
   a) Ensure good governance
   b) Make contract enforcement easier and faster
   c) Establish alternative conflict resolution mechanisms
   d) Guarantee property protection
   e) Reduce the bankruptcy stigma and facilitate re-starts.
4. **Guide entrepreneurs through the Startup administrative process and enhance the benefits of formalization**
   a) Carry out information campaigns on regulatory requirements
   b) Make explicit the link between regulatory requirements and public services, including business support services
   c) Assist start-ups in meeting regulatory requirements

14.4 ENABLING ECOSYSTEM - INTERNATIONAL COMPARISONS

We have brought together a set of metrics relating to a set of factors for select countries to represent the regulatory and socio-economic environment having a bearing on an enabling ecosystem for promoting entrepreneurship.

India's scores relating to most parameters are pathetic. It is a miracle that entrepreneurial businesses flower amidst such somewhat hostile environment; surely, a tribute to the genius, hardiness and resilience of the Indian entrepreneur.

We should acknowledge that the process of arriving at these rankings is not precisely science. And, therefore, these indices need not reflect accurately the relative levels of comparable values for the different parameters for different countries. There could be subjective elements at play. India's poor ranking relating to parameters like corruption perception or economic freedom should be taken with some caution. India's boisterous democracy with a nosy, aggressive press and opposition "... *trumpet its scams and scandals more than happens in, say, China.*"

India's poor ranking, nevertheless, point to the long distance the country has yet to cover before our policies and governance create a liberal and competitive economic environment. Indian entrepreneurs have done exceptionally well in some countries, which offer the right environment.

a) About 80% of all polished diamonds sold worldwide pass through Indian hands. Indian diamond dealers energized the jewelry districts in New York, Hong Kong and Antwerp.

b) Indian-Americans (almost entirely originating from the State of Gujarat in India) own more than 22,000 hotels in the US representing over 50% lodging properties in the economy segment and almost 40% of all hotel properties.

c) California, home to the best and the brightest entrepreneurs from around the world operating on the cutting-edge of technology, has about 3000 companies owned by Indian entrepreneurs.

d) Sweden's biggest hotelier is Bicky Chakraborty.

e) The World Startup Report 2013 states that 62% of US Startups are rumoured to have Indian Co-founders.

Asian entrepreneurs, with significant representation from Indian Diaspora, are at the cutting edge of the British entrepreneurial community. Asian wealth in the UK has become exceedingly diverse, across generations, spanning manufacturing and services, entertainment and fashion, hotels and property and food and pharmaceuticals. These entrepreneurial initiatives *"successfully combined the dynamism of the free market with the go-getting, risk-taking heroism of the entrepreneur."*

The international comparisons are based on the following reports: Doing Business Index 2015; The Global Competitiveness Report, 2015–16; Global Entrepreneurship and Development Index (GEDI), 2015; Corruption Perceptions Index, 2015; The 2015 Index of Economic Freedom; The Global Innovation Index, 2015; and The Baseline Profitability Index 2015.

EASE OF DOING BUSINESS 2015, WORLD BANK (doingbusiness.org/rankings)

If entrepreneurs were to pursue smart ideas, which drive economic development, sound business regulations – good rules, which are efficient, accessible to all and simple in their implementation – are critical.

This ranking assesses the extent of obstacles to doing business in relation to a set of regulations affecting 11 areas of life of a business: Starting a business, dealing with construction permits, registering property, getting electricity, getting credit, protecting investors, paying taxes, trading across borders, enforcing contract, closing a business or resolving insolvency. A high ease of doing business rank means the regulatory environment is more conducive to the starting and operation of a local firm.

Out of the 189 countries studied, India's rank in 2015 was 130, jumping 12 places from the earlier year. However, countries like Iran, Uganda, Lebanon or West Bank & Gaza are ahead of India.

The number of days it takes to register a company in select countries: New Zealand - 0.5 days; US - 5.6 days; Iran - 15 days; India - 29 days; China - 31.4 days. India's ranks are terrible for dealing with construction permits (183), enforcing contracts (178), paying taxes (157) and starting business (155). India has done well for indicators such as protecting minority investors (8) and ensuring credit (42).

It takes about 4.3 years, on average, to resolve a bankruptcy case in India, more than twice as long as in China. (The recently introduced legal framework should ease the situation considerably.)

GLOBAL COMPETITIVENESS REPORT, 2015–16
(WORLD ECONOMIC FORUM, GENEVA - www.weforum.org)

The report defines competitiveness in terms of "... *the set of institutions, policies and factors that determine the level of productivity of a country.*" The level of productivity, in turn, determines the level of prosperity that an economy can generate.

The report tracks/measures 12 pillars of economic competitiveness like institutions, infrastructure, macro-economic environment, higher education and training, market efficiency and technological readiness. Rankings are calculated from both publicly available data and the Executive Opinion Survey, a comprehensive annual survey conducted by the WEF together with its network of Partner Institutions in the countries covered by the report.

India ranks 55 among the 140 countries studied. Countries like China, Brazil, Indonesia and South Africa are ahead of India. Barring Financial Market Development (India's rank being 53) and Innovation and Sophistication factors (46), India's scores for other parameters are extremely low. Despite all the reforms of recent times, India's rank for the number of procedures required to start a business is as low as 129.

CORRUPTION PERCEPTIONS INDEX, 2015
(www.transparency.org/cpi)

Burdensome bureaucracy and corruption can be a major disincentive for entrepreneurial endeavors. Complicated ex-ante approvals as well as ex-post regulatory oversight (burdensome tax compliance, employment regulations etc.) are deterrents.

The Index reflects what the public at large perceives about the quality of public governance (which should ideally put the interests of its citizens first) of each country on the basis of opinion surveys.

This, of course, cannot be considered a very objective measure in relative terms. In a boisterous, free democracy like India, public frustration can be louder than that in not-so-free countries.

India's rank for 2015 is 76 out of 168 countries surveyed. India earned a low score of 38 on a scale of 0 (most corrupt) to 100 (least corrupt). However, India's score improved in 2015 from 85 in 2014.

THE 2015 INDEX OF ECONOMIC FREEDOM
(THE HERITAGE FOUNDATION, USA - www.heritage.org)

There is a positive relationship between economic freedom and prosperity. Countries with greater economic freedom have higher per capita GDP. Economic freedom is highly correlated with innovation and entrepreneurial dynamism.

The Index is a composite measure of 10 components of economic freedom grouped into four broad categories or pillars of economic freedom:

1. Rule of Law (property rights, freedom from corruption)
2. Limited government (fiscal freedom, government spending)

3. Regulatory efficiency (business freedom, labour freedom, monetary freedom)
4. Open markets (trade, investments, financial freedom)

Countries are graded as free, mostly free, moderately free, and mostly unfree and repressed. Among the 178 countries graded, India's rank is 128 slightly ahead of China, both under the category of mostly unfree.

THE GLOBAL INNOVATION INDEX, 2015
(globalinnovationindex.org)

INSEAD, the French Business School, Cornell University and World Intellectual Property Organization construct the GII. The GII recognizes the paramount role of innovation in economic growth and prosperity.

The index has been prepared for 141 countries and India's overall rank is 81, lower than other BRIC countries. For Innovation Input (Sub-Index), India's rank is 100, Innovation Output rank is 69 and for Innovation Efficiency Ratio the rank is 11. IE ratio is calculated as the ratio of the output over the Input sub-Index. India has done well in 6 out of the 7 key indicators: the citable documents, the QS university ranking, high-tech and medium high-tech output, GERD (Gross Domestic Expenditure on R&D) performed by business enterprises over GDP, logistics performance and patent families filed in at least 3 offices (Relates to 2014).

Innovation Input reflects Institutions for which India's rank is 106 (of which Press Freedom, the rank is 115, obviously a flawed ranking); Regulatory Environment - 83; Business Environment - 128; Human Capital and Research - 96 (of which the rank for education is 128 and R&D 31); General Infrastructure - 87; Market Sophistication - 50; Business Sophistication - 93; and Trade and Competition - 106 (Relates to 2014).

Innovation Output: Knowledge & Technology Outputs 50 and Creative Outputs 82.

For domestic resident patent applications, India's rank is 52 whereas that of China is 1 (Of course, the quality of many of these patents is reportedly worthless) (Relates to 2014).

THE BASELINE PROFITABILITY INDEX 2015

INDIA ON TOP OF THE WORLD!

Daniel Altman, Adjunct Professor, Stern School of Business, New York University, has created the index. The ranking is based on an index for baseline profitability that assumes that 3 factors impact the ultimate success of a foreign investment:

1. How much the value of an asset grows?
2. The preservation of that value while the asset is owned.
3. The ease of repatriation of proceeds from selling the asset.

The index combines measures for each of these factors into a summary statistic that conveys a country's basic attractiveness for investment. A high ranking points to high returns and improving economic institutions. The index, thus, compares how local policies and conditions have a bearing on the same investment in different countries.

India is ranked first. The rankings of USA, South Africa, China, Brazil and Russia are respectively 50, 51, 65, 99 and 105 among 110 countries. Prof. Altman admits that the calculation of the BPI is an imperfect exercise fraught with assumptions.

15
Promoting Small Businesses: Policy Aids

"... The role of governments in nurturing and protecting one of the most important engines of growth – entrepreneurs – has never been more important. For the past 25 years, these business leaders have done more than any other group to stimulate innovation and create jobs during periods of prosperity and in more challenging economic conditions." - Entrepreneurs Speak Out 2012, Ernst & Young report

15.1 CRITICAL NEEDS OF SMALL BUSINESSES

1. An enabling business environment
2. Capacity building
3. Access to capital (equity and debt)
4. Access to information and technology
5. Access to infrastructure

1. AN ENABLING BUSINESS ENVIRONMENT

Many World Bank studies demonstrate that cumbersome entry regulation is associated with less private investment, higher consumer prices, greater administrative corruption and a larger informal economy.

In most instances, the entrepreneur himself ends up wasting precious time on such activities denying him time for more productive activities. Small businesses have limited staff to handle such issues.

The only way the administrative burdens can be contained is by simplifying and speeding up administrative procedures. Many countries have improved legal, financial and regulatory frameworks, cutting through red tape and reporting requirements, tax compliance burdens, reforming employment protection legislation by, among other things, easing inflexible procedures.

Financial incentives, marketing support, low-cost consulting services etc are part of an enabling environment.

2. CAPACITY BUILDING

Teaching entrepreneurship has been a popular initiative of the governments of many countries. Apparently, there is no single model for teaching entrepreneurship, assuming for a moment that entrepreneurship can be taught. The fundamental issue is:

Should young people be taught how to start their own business? Or should we address a more fundamental issue, strengthening their resolve to take risks?

USA tends to favor the former approach while Sweden prefers the latter. UK uses both approaches. Entrepreneurship education at the University level is advanced and popular in the US. Europe is attempting to teach business and entrepreneurship at the school level.

3. ACCESS TO CAPITAL (EQUITY AND DEBT)

The policy support is aimed at reducing the high risk profile of small businesses by directing policies at easing access to financing; increased support for debt financing through loans and loan guarantees; helping access risk capital at all stages of development, preferably on liberal terms. UNCTAD has provided a checklist of key questions related to improving access to finance for Startups. This is available at the following URL - unctad.org/en/PublicationsLibrary/diaeed2012d1_en.pdf.

4. ACCESS TO INFORMATION AND TECHNOLOGY

A budding entrepreneur requires a huge amount of reliable, updated information on a wide range of issues - regulatory requirements, access to finance, market intelligence, source of technology, networking possibilities etc. A comprehensive website maintained by government agencies and industry associations could be a less expensive and more impactful option.

In the area of technology, the range of assistance could be:

a) Increasing the participation of small businesses in research networks and technology markets.

b) Supporting the emergence of innovative clusters.

c) Enhancing the awareness of IP system - patents, copyright and trademark.

d) ICT-driven investments such as e-government and web portals.

5. ACCESS TO INFRASTRUCTURE

Land and quality infrastructure including accommodation for industrial workers are a major problem, particularly in cities both for large as well as small businesses. Inadequacies of hard infrastructure – roads, utilities, real estates, logistics etc. – increase the transaction cost disproportionately for new businesses and act as a distraction from core business operations.

Technology Business Incubators – providing general and technical infrastructure, advisory, mentoring, networking, accessing information, facilitating access to Venture Capital all under one roof – are emerging as a powerful platform for promoting innovative Startups. The number of such Incubators is over 1300 in USA & Canada, over 800 in China, 300 in South Korea and 200 in Japan. India has only about 115 Incubators most of which have been setup by National Science and Technology Entrepreneurship Development Board, Department of Science and Technology, Government of India.

Technopreneurship Promotion Programme (TePP) has been India's largest network programme supporting independent innovators. TePP, an initiative of the Ministry of Science and Technology, has 30 outreach centers spread across the country, which provide grants, technical guidance and mentoring support. Funds are provided in two phases: Innovation incubation up to Rs. 1.5 million and Enterprise incubation up to Rs. 5 million.

15.2 AGGRESSIVE PUBLIC POLICIES PROMOTING INCUBATORS IN INDIA

LIVELIHOOD BUSINESS INCUBATORS (LBIs)

LBIs are low technology/livelihood incubators designed as part of a favourable ecosystem for creating jobs at local level, thereby, reducing rural unemployment. They encourage those commercial activities, which are need-based to create enterprises in the rural area.

LBIs will promote Business Incubators in various skills and those who acquire the skills will have the opportunity to set up their own business enterprises. In other words, LBIs aim to achieve two things at one go: Skill development training to youths and promotion of enterprises by them. LBIs will also make available mentoring and handholding and financial support.

National Small Industries Corporation, Khadi and Village Commission and Coir Board or any other institution of Govt. of India/State Governments will be the public agencies supporting the initiative. Private partners can also set up LBIs under PPP mode with the above public agencies.

TECHNOLOGY BUSINESS INCUBATORS (TBIS)

Technology-driven new enterprises are typically high-risk, high-growth ventures requiring an enabling environment like TBI to improve the chances of success. The objective of the TBI, an initiative of the Ministry of MSMEs, for new enterprise creation based on new technology or knowledge, include:

a) Incubating innovative ideas/technology in the agro-based industry.

b) Providing a platform for speedy commercialization of technologies developed in any industry

c) Interfacing and networking; networking among academia, industry and financial institutions

d) Value addition; providing value added services like legal, financial, technical and IPR to incubatees.

TBIs, acting as a growth driver in the low-end spectrum of the incubation ecosystem, will focus on those technologies, which need support for commercialization and proliferation. The services offered by a TBI will cover: Mentoring, Business Plans, networking of business resources, choosing the appropriate technology, project/product choice, project report preparation, credit facilitation, Seed Capital assistance and marketing assistance. Industry associations, academic institutions, R&D labs, Technology Parks etc. could promote TBIs. Minimum built-up space shall be 5000 sq. ft.

The funding assistance covers:

a) Capital grants for plant & machinery

b) Grants for supporting ideas: Rs. 0.2 million per idea to be released after selection by the Local Screening cum Expert Committee

c) Seed Capital Fund for the creation of enterprises: Rs 4.0 million as first installment; Rs. 3.0 million after 70% of first installment has been disbursed and utilized; Rs. 3.0 million as the last installment.

d) For holding Accelerator Workshop to provide holistic support to the incubatees/participants: Rs.2.0 million per workshop

e) Fund of Funds to be managed by SIDBI: Rs. 600 million to be deployed to promote technology and business incubators

Select Incubators in India (Other than TePP) include Centre for Innovation Incubation an Entrepreneurship, IIM Ahmadabad; Society for Innovation and Entrepreneurship, IIT Bombay; Wadhwani Centre for Entrepreneurship Development, ISB, Hyderabad; Science and Technology Entrepreneurship Park, IIT Kharagpur; Technology Business Incubator, IIT Delhi; Technology Business Incubator, Technopark, Trivandrum; Gen Next Innovation Hub, Mumbai (promoted by Reliance Industries and Microsoft); GSF Accelerator, Gurgaon; Venture Nursery, Mumbai and Kyron Accelerator, Chennai. Multinational corporations like Target, Coca-Cola and Pitney Bowes have launched Acceleration programmes in India.

15.3 UNCTAD'S REPORT FOR NATIONAL POLICYMAKERS & REGULATORS

UNCTAD's Entrepreneurship Policy Framework and Implementation Guidance report has provided guidelines and checklists of questions as a guide for policymakers and regulatory bodies for:

1. Formulating National Entrepreneurship Strategy
2. Optimizing the Regulatory Environment
3. Enhancing Entrepreneurship Education and Skills Development
4. Facilitating Technology Exchange and Innovation
5. Improving Access to Finance
6. Promoting Awareness and Networking

The UNCTAD Report, which also provides Indicators to Measure Effectiveness of Entrepreneurship Policies, can be downloaded using the following link: unctad.org/en/PublicationsLibrary/diaeed2012d1_en.pdf

15.4 USA - AN ENTREPRENEURIAL HOTHOUSE: WHY AND HOW

"... Entrepreneurship (is) central to American culture, may be literally a part of the DNA (thanks to all of those immigrants importing the gene that makes you get up and go.)" - Lexington, The Economist, June 19, 2010

About 70% of all Americans report that they have considered starting their own business. In Europe this ratio is only 40%. At any point, about 10% of the working population in the US is engaged in the process of creating a nascent business; this ratio is less than 4% for most European countries and below 2% for Japan and France.

America's corporate and personal bankruptcy systems are the most generous in the world. This leniency encourages the failed entrepreneurs to try, try again. In Silicon Valley, executives proudly make their failed Startup the centerpiece of their resume.

"If you start a company in London or Paris and go bust, you have just ruined your future; do it in Silicon Valley and you have simply completed your entrepreneurial learning. In Europe those who go bankrupt tend to be considered as losers. They face great difficulty to finance a new venture." - Communication by the European Commission, 1998

One of the great contributing factors to the astounding flowering of entrepreneurship has been US's openness to outsiders *"Émigrés have always been more entrepreneurial than their stay-at-home cousins: the three most entrepreneurial spaces in modern history have been the ones inhabited by the Jewish, Chinese and Indian diasporas."* - The Economist, March 14, 2009

Foreigners are only about 12.5% of the total US population; but high tech Startups with immigrant founders account for 25%. That is, immigrants are more than twice as likely to start businesses as their native-born counterparts. In fact, this proportion is around 50% in Silicon Valley. Immigrants founded 40% of the US's Fortune 500 firms.

The *'economically innovative and civically vibrant community'* that Cuban immigrants have created in their new homeland - Miami, USA - has been a compelling validation of how the environment can help leverage entrepreneurial energies for the benefit of the community as a whole. In contrast, their compatriots back home lead a life of deprivation.

INSTITUTIONAL SUPPORT

Wide-ranging institutional support, light regulatory processes and pro-enterprise labour laws represent a remarkable feature of the US scene. The entrepreneurship support programme prevailing in the US is exceedingly broad-based and creative. A study done by the Kauffman Foundation identified the following core components of the programme on the basis of a survey of existing entrepreneurs:

1. An enabling entrepreneurial ecosystem to facilitate easy access to knowledge/information, capital, talent and networks.

2. Peer-to-peer mentoring and consulting advice provided by other entrepreneurs from non-competing activities - identified as one of the top "best practices" entrepreneurship support programme. *"Peers help identify entrepreneurial opportunities, influence perceptions about entrepreneurship as a career choice and serve as good substitute for direct experience."*

3. Promoting partnerships: Under a Business Retention and Expansion Strategy, companies at risk are identified in a community and assistance is provided to overcome economic difficulties to avoid shutting down their operations by networking with professionals, support groups and local government officials.

4. Easing the regulatory process: Streamlining regulatory and licensing processes is considered the most cost-effective and

quickest approach a region can take to support entrepreneurial activity.

5. Raising capital
6. Commercializing innovation

Founded in 1953, the Small Business Administration (SBA) has delivered millions of loans, loan guarantees, contracts, counseling sessions and other forms of assistance to small businesses. The four broad programmatic functions are: Access to capital, entrepreneurial development (education, information, technical assistance and training), Government contracting and advocacy for, among other things, reducing the negative impact of regulations on small businesses.

OTHER UNIQUE BUSINESS ENABLERS

1. **Accelerators/Incubators**: These are Startup schools, which are sprouting in cities across the world, heavily concentrated in the US. They provide:

   a) The minimum physical facilities to launch a Startup
   b) Technical, legal and other mentoring services
   c) Access to network of contacts
   d) A stamp of approval
   e) Help to source funding

   Some of the successful Accelerators/Incubators in the USA are Y-Combinator in Silicon Valley, TechStars and The Founder Institute.

2. **Startup Labs/Events**: There are a number of Startup Labs and Startup Events where developers, designers, marketers, product managers and Startup enthusiasts are brought together to share ideas, form teams, build products and launch Startups. These help aspiring entrepreneurs to arrive at viable business models. Kauffman Labs for Enterprise Creation and SU Labs are two of the highly successful labs; Startup Weekends represent a popular event where entrepreneurs come together to set up Startups.

3. **Centres for Entrepreneurship**: An interesting phenomenon in the US has been the promotion of Centres for Entrepreneurship

as a bridge between academia and business community. Wealthy entrepreneurs create Centres in their names. *"What pyramids were to Egyptian rulers, named Centres are to entrepreneurs. Endowing a centre at a University is the modern key to immortality!"*

These Centers provide Incubation support like low rent, consulting, communication network, seminar or forums for prospective entrepreneurs and investors and business plan competition with decent prize money.

4. **Crowdfunding**: The US offers fertile soil for the sprouting of such ideas. Crowdfunding originated as a way to raise money for creative projects presented on websites. This model allows thousands of potential users of a service, buyers of a product or art lovers to invest in ideas that excite them. The money they give is a vote of confidence in the project. Initially, the typical project raised $5000 supported by 85 people. But it could also be as large as $10.3 million raised by Pebble, a smart watch that uses electronic-ink technology. Kickstarter.com, the most popular website engaged in crowd funding of the new ideas, is today a $2.8 billion global firm.

15.5 THE INDIAN SCENE: THE STUPENDOUS CHALLENGES

Despite the recent upsurge in the growth of Startups in India, at the basic level of innovation and entrepreneurship the country has a lot of catching up to do. Deficits in human capital, R&D, infrastructure and knowledge and technology outputs continue to penalize the innovation front in the country. India's rank as per Global Entrepreneurship and Development Index is as low as 89 (out of the 118 countries studied) India's rank is below China, Russia and Egypt. The ranking for innovation was equally bad.

According to the Global Entrepreneurship Monitor, early stage entrepreneurial activity (as a percentage of adult population) in India in the recent past has been less than 10% compared to over 14% in China.

Although Indian economy has undergone an impressive transformation during the past 25 years, the share of unorganized sector remained stubbornly persistent. Lack of reliable and updated data on this unorganized, informal sector renders the process of designing and delivering appropriate strategies for strengthening the Micro and Small enterprises difficult.

Lack of formal employment opportunities and poverty are pushing a large number of people into entrepreneurial activities ranging from street vending to traditional personal services. Reportedly, India has the highest rate of shadow economy entrepreneurship in the world. Self-employment rates are highest among the lower income levels. Such micro enterprises operate at a subsistence level in the informal sector characterized by poor productivity and low efficiency. They do not create high-quality jobs nor enhance competitiveness through innovations. In fact, most such **necessity-driven entrepreneurs** of such enterprises abandon their businesses as soon as they get full-time employment.

According to the Ministry of MSME, Govt. of India, *"The sector is a blend of tradition and modern with an alarming level of informal sector enterprises at the bottom of the MSME pyramid."* But then, we should not lose sight of the fact that such enterprises, most belonging to the self-employment category, are a source of employment and income for vulnerable populations.

As against such not-so-impressive evidence, there are the inspirational success stories of first-generation Indian entrepreneurs who created large scale direct as well as indirect employment and huge wealth for themselves and for the society at large: Reliance, HCL, Cognizant, Infosys, Hero and Bharti Group are examples. (In fact, quite a few of the currently large enterprises even in developed countries started out as micro and small family businesses).

WEAK ENTREPRENEURIAL ECOSYSTEM

Despite improvements over the years, the entrepreneurial ecosystem available in India compares poorly even with many developing countries, as was evident from the international comparisons presented earlier. It is not precisely conducive to accelerating entrepreneurial growth.

Four-fifths of the jobs in Indian manufacturing are in firms employing less than 50 workers. Firms wanting to grow larger have problems dealing with troublesome regulators, buying land, securing power and working around the country's complicated labour laws. Till recently, the labour market was subjected to around 250 labour rules at the Centre and State levels.

"*At present, we find many gaps in the policy and regulatory framework which inhibit rather than promote entrepreneurship.*" - Creating a Vibrant Entrepreneurial Ecosystem in India, Planning Commission, Govt. of India

World Economic Forum is forthright on this aspect as it relates to India: "*Entrepreneurship cannot thrive in environments where regulation is too rigid and where more barriers than opportunities are embedded in the business creation process. To help entrepreneurs unleash their potential, the regulatory environment in India needs to encourage firms to formally start up and grow. An appropriate regulatory framework should ensure fair competition, better access to markets and trade negotiations that ensure a level playing field for domestic manufacturers, review of existing regulations, and reduction in the burden of paper work and procedures.*"

The sources of the five most problematic factors for doing business in India as identified by World Economic Forum's Executive Opinion Survey were: **Inadequate supply of infrastructure, inefficient government bureaucracy, corruption, restrictive regulations** and **access to financing**.

According to World Startup Report, 2013, Indian infrastructure currently stands at Chinese's 1990 levels, IPO at 2000 levels and Internet at 2006 levels. Poorly planned roads, inefficient logistics, slow and unreliable Internet, numerous outages in water supply, frequent power cuts are some of the issues raised in the report.

The complexity and unpredictability of the process of accessing even what the Government offers to MSMEs tend to be high.

Unless India takes on the tasks of removing barriers to entry on a war footing – offering an operating environment which is accountable, transparent, efficient and predictable, and making the business exit process more efficient and less costly – there is no way the country can promote entrepreneurship on a scale warranted.

ACCESS TO FUNDING, A CRITICAL BARRIER

Over 90% of the MSMEs are outside the coverage of formal financial channels.(In fact, one estimate indicates that MSMEs get less than 5% of its credit needs from the formal banking system). These businesses are largely self-financed or rely on personal networks or money lenders.

Angel investor funding and VC financing have been weak and more efforts need to be made to align investors' resources with enterprise ideas.

Inadequate flow of risk capital deters high potential individuals from becoming entrepreneurs. According to CII, one of the biggest hurdles for SME growth is non-availability of affordable, adequate and timely finance for modernization, expansion, diversification, partnerships and international collaborations as well as to buy or import quality raw materials and technology.

This scenario can change significantly with the recent (June 2015) easing of regulatory issues; Securities and Exchange Board of India relaxed norms for fund-raising and IPOs for Startups.

Promoters of Startups are generally considered too risky to be funded by conventional financial institutions due to a variety of factors: Young entrepreneurs have typically little or no asset to provide as collateral; untested or unproven business model; likelihood of failure; high administrative costs of servicing SMEs relative to their level of funding; and difficulties of obtaining valid credit information on such businesses.

Stringent lending guidelines and risk-averse nature of financial institutions compel many SMEs to depend on informal sources of capital like relatives or moneylenders. According to the latest Census of MSMEs, only 5.2% avail finance from institutional sources, 2.1% finance from non-institutional sources. Over 92% of the units had no outside finance, essentially depending on self-finance, which can impose serious limitations.

The National Knowledge Commission's assessment of early stage finance in the country gives a different set of figures: 63% - own funds (47% of which borrowed from family and friends), 22% - Banks, 9% - State Financial Corporations and 3% - each from Angels and Venture Capitalists.

The capital shortage (the difference between what is required and what is available) is severe in the case of Micro enterprises.

Strengthening publically-funded Credit Guarantee Schemes (underwriting the risk of lending to SMEs by reimbursing the banks either in full or in part in the event of a default on loan), extending the Performance and Credit Rating Scheme to cover more MSMEs (facilitating easy access to credit under favorable terms) and expanding Factoring Services by banks and non-banking finance companies are some of the suggestions made by the Working Group on MSMEs, Planning Commission, Government of India.

Severe regulatory restrictions acted as a deterrent to the larger flow of Venture Capital or Angel Funds. Lack of equity support limits the leveraging capacity for raising additional debt. The situation, however, has been improving lately following appropriate policy interventions.

The Committee on Creating a Vibrant Entrepreneurial Ecosystem in India, 2012 affirms that promoting a massive entrepreneurial base to generate the required level of employment is predicated on massive infusion of capital, equity and debt, through Angel Investors, Incubators, VC Funds and banks and financial institutions. The Committee had estimated that the capital required to promote entrepreneurship during the period 2012–22 would be about Rs. 3 trillion, half of which in the form of debt.

CAPACITY BUILDING

In India, entrepreneurship development programmes of varying duration and quality have vigorously been pursued in all the States for several years. The effectiveness of such programmes – the number of participants of such programmes promoting successful enterprises – is uncertain; the general impression is that the success rate is poor.

Funding workforce-training schemes has been extensively pursued in many countries. In India, the National Skill Development Council is spearheading a massive public-private initiative.

The National Institute for Entrepreneurship and Business Development was formed under the Ministry of Micro, Small and Medium Enterprises, Govt. of India. It is engaged in creating an environment conducive to the development of entrepreneurship and a favorable attitude amongst the general public to support those who opt for an entrepreneurial career by removing the prevalent misconceptions or prejudices. Visit http://www.niesbud.nic.in/ for more details.

INFRASTRUCTURE AVAILABILITY

There are serious gaps in the range and quality of infrastructure available to MSMEs sector at affordable cost across the country. We fail to recognize that availability of good quality infrastructure enhances the competitiveness of enterprises, big or small. Maintenance of Industrial Estates/Areas (roads, drainage, power distribution, water supply, common effluent treatment plants, common facilities etc.) has been thoroughly inadequate. World over, modern enterprises are housed in Modular Industrial Estates having raw material banks, technology resource centres, design centres, business centres and trade fair centres.

A recent strategic intervention pursued by public authorities for promoting micro and small enterprises has been cluster-based programmes (some industry-specific), which optimize the cost of providing/accessing a variety of facilities and services.

MSMEs IN THE MANUFACTURING SECTOR

Estimated number of such units is nearly 12 million, of which 99% are micro enterprises, mostly one-person affairs in the informal sector. These units face extreme challenges: Difficulties of accessing formal finance at reasonable rates, absence of business advisory at affordable cost on improving operational efficiency or expanding market and unhelpful, if not hostile, attitude of regulatory authorities are some of the issues these units have to live with.

The greatest need of the hour is helping promote millions of such units to generate millions of entry-level factory jobs to accommodate the millions of unskilled and semi-skilled youths annually joining the labour pool in the next few decades in the country.

ENSURING SYSTEMIC ROBUSTNESS

The Report on Creating Vibrant Entrepreneurial Ecosystem highlights the need for enablers such as catalytic Government policy and regulatory environment, easy access to capital and hard infrastructure, established businesses fostering entrepreneurship and providing source of exits, a culture which stimulates risk-taking and collaboration forums to connect various stake holders.

There is an urgent need to address the problem of the absence of a suitable mechanism that enables the quick revival of viable sick enterprises and allows unviable entities to close down speedily. A new bill was introduced in December 2015 to overhaul the bankruptcy framework to allow speedy winding up of failed businesses to protect the interests of shareholders and lenders. The Bankruptcy and Law Reform Commission proposed insolvency resolution within 180 days.

Low technology levels and inadequate access to modern technology is an issue to be addressed. Leveraging the power of IT would be essential if SMEs have to play a larger role. Currently, a mere 1% of India's MSMEs are incorporating ICT for business.

Multiplicity of labour laws and complicated procedures associated with compliance of such laws act as a drag on small businesses. If we are serious about supporting small businesses, these should be streamlined right away. Enhancing strategic capability by providing services including business consulting to deliver business planning, marketing schemes, productivity growth etc. at low cost or no cost at all by promotional agencies of the government and industry associations has been pursued in many countries.

Analysts of global trends believe that India should learn a lesson or two from the Chinese success story:

a) Chinese talents returning home from Taiwan, Singapore and US account for many of the country's entrepreneurial successes.

b) Indian diaspora has a rich pool of high-quality entrepreneurial talents. It is reported that Indians account for 15% of Startups in Silicon Valley; another estimate indicates that Indians are co-promoters of 25% of Startups in Silicon Valley (The estimates may vary as between different sources, but all agree that the contribution of Indians to the success of tech Startups in Silicon Valley has been significant.) Attracting them home should be the goal of high priority. This goal can be accomplished only if we replicate the environment in which such non-resident entrepreneurs/professionals bloomed. The first step towards creating an attractive investment climate is getting rid of mindless bureaucratic and regulatory restrictions.

National Entrepreneurship Policy document of India distinguishes between 'hard' policy instruments and 'soft' policy instruments. The former directly benefits established firms. The latter includes awareness promotion, skill development, networking and mentoring, collectively strengthening the mindset of the target groups.

"Innovation and entrepreneurship have become two of the most important sources of competitive advantage. Building these capabilities will represent a fundamental challenge for the country in the coming years." - Baba Kalyani, CMD, Bharat Forge Limited.

PART IV

Business Opportunity Identification and Screening

16
Business Opportunity Identification

16.1 BROAD OPTIONS FOR A NEW BUSINESS

1. Promoting a Startup: Follow your dream
2. Buying an existing business: Advantage of having current customers and a known record of performance. Potential rewards depend on a range of factors including the lifecycle phase of the industry.
3. Franchising: Advantages being brand recognition, lower marketing costs, support from the principals.

16.2 BUSINESS IDEA GENERATION

For an entrepreneur, a business opportunity is the chance to do something, which is both different and better than the way it is done now, delivering new value to the customer.

The process underlying idea generation is the formation of new pattern of parts that already exists. *"No idea creates anything out of nothing. It essentially uncovers, selects, reshuffles, combines, synthesizes already existing facts or ideas or facilities or skills."* - Arthur Koesler, *The Act of Creation*

In fact, Thomas Edison didn't invent light bulbs. The stable, cheap filament, the glass container, the vacuum pump were in the making for 77 years. Of course, Edison had the genius to integrate them.

Every business opportunity is based on an idea; all ideas are not business opportunities, however. *"Opportunities are ideas that have been through an analytical wringer. Take an idea, punch it, pull it, ask the right questions, and, if it holds up, it is an opportunity to build a viable venture."*

The difference between an idea and an opportunity is whether:

a) You can build it and get it into the market.

b) There are enough customers who are willing and have the purchasing power to buy the product at a price which generates adequate profits.

c) You are confident to deal with the level of the prevailing or potential competition.

Most entrepreneurs start their business by copying or marginally modifying ideas created by someone else. Some replicate or modify ideas that they came across when they were employed. Some, of course, discover the idea by chance or serendipity; and a few at the end of a single-minded pursuit. Identifying viable business ideas is as much an art or matter of luck as the use of systematic techniques.

For a Startup, the search starts with you. Your:

a) Educational/professional background

b) Expertise, interests and personal qualities

c) Financial strength

d) External contacts/resources

16.3 TECHNIQUES FOR IDEA GENERATION

1. FOUR INNOVATION STYLES (https://innovationstyles.com/isinc/styles/overview.aspx)

1. *Visioning*: Imagining an ideal future and letting long-term goals envision and idealize; use intuition, insights and images.

2. *Exploring*: Questioning/challenging the assumptions and discovering novel possibilities.

3. *Experimenting*: Testing out various combinations of new ideas and learning from the results.

4. *Modifying*: Refining, optimizing and improving what has already been done.

2. ENTREPRENEURIAL INSIGHTS

G.T. Lumpkin, Hans Hansen and Jeremy Short of the Texas Technology University, in their book *Understanding Entrepreneurial Insights: Frontiers of Entrepreneurship Research,* have isolated the following insights for identifying new opportunities:

1. *Problem-solving insights: Emanate from and systematic approach to solving a problem.*
2. *Tinkering insights: This is a moment of surprise when the activity is unplanned, making do with the materials and knowledge at hand.*
3. *Abductive insights: They are at the heart of "eureka" moments that come as a flash; the discovery process could be nearly mystical, inspired, serendipitous or as a result of superior intellect or just plain luck.*

3. INTERACTING WITH PROSPECTIVE CUSTOMERS

One-to-one discussions or focus group discussions with prospective customers can throw up possibilities.

4. FOUR QUADRANTS GRID

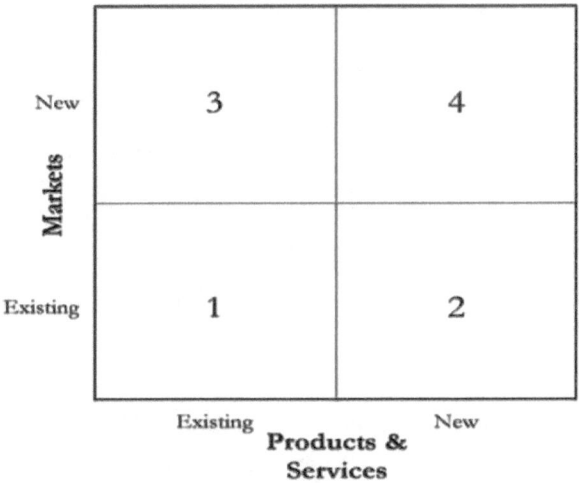

1. Simplest ideas to be located in box 1 but the risk being severe competition.
2. Ideas with the most unpredictable outcomes (a winner or a loser) and most difficult to pull off are likely to be in box 4.
3. Look closely at the combination in boxes 2 & 3 to identify interesting possibilities both in terms of growth opportunities and profit margins.

16.4 SOURCES OF NEW IDEAS

1. MAKING CHANGES TO EXISTING PRODUCTS

1. Make them larger, smaller, lighter, heavier, faster, slower
2. Change their color, material or shape
3. Alter their quality or quantity
4. Increase mobility, access, portability, disposability
5. Simplify repair, maintenance, replacement, cleaning
6. Introduce automation, simplification, convenience
7. Add new features, accessories
8. Change the delivery method, packaging, unit size, shape
9. Improve usability, safety
10. Broaden/narrow the range
11. Improve service

2. APPLYING THE SCAMPER QUESTIONS TO A GIVEN SITUATION (mindtools.com)

Substitute (other ingredients, materials) or simplify/**C**ombine or condense/**A**dapt or alter/ **M**odify or magnify or miniaturize/**P**ut to other uses/**E**liminate or expand/**R**earrange or reverse.

Example: Unwanted clothes – Combine with other things to make life-sized dolls or scarecrow; alter size/color/shape, dye and remodel; make trousers into shorts; use as a substitute for padding for cushions, dust covers or blankets; use to provide fancy dress; recycle or reuse.

3. THOSE BASED ON EXISTING RESOURCES

Those based on natural resources and existing industrial base offer possibilities with backward/forward linkages.

Example: Exploiting marine resources in a region yields opportunities for building boats or making nets (backward linkages) and for ice factories, can-making units, refrigerated vehicles etc. (forward linkages).

4. NEW KNOWLEDGE

Knowledge and technology-based: IT, Biotechnology, new medicines, wind or solar energy- related products, hybrid cars, new electronic products etc.

5. GOVERNMENT POLICY CHANGES

Examples include the deregulation of telephone industry in India that opened up several possibilities and the new "Make in India" programme which is giving a boost to the manufacturing sector.

6. CIVIC FAILURE

a) Perception of rising crime rates: Car alarms, home security.

b) Poor electricity supply generates demand for Inverter business.

c) Failure of delivery of quality education in the public system leads to the growth of private institutions. When organized systems can't meet the demand, especially for higher education, unorganized institutions like parallel colleges mushroom.

7. DEMAND/MARKET-DRIVEN OPPORTUNITIES

1. The telltale signs of market opportunities include: High growth rate of the market for the product; high margins; unfulfilled customer needs; market not segmented; few or weak competitors; competitors' slow response to changing market requirements; spotty product availability; and low threat of substitute products.

2. Filling an unmet need or create the need in the market place with a new product.

3. Delivering additional value to the customer by producing better quality product or at lower costs or providing more flexibility in the way it is delivered, often deploying a new technology.
4. Export opportunities
5. Quest for convenient solutions: Cooked food, child-care
6. Changing tastes
7. Opportunities which big companies ignore
8. Import substitution possibilities

8. LOOK FOR PROBLEMS

Instead of chasing ideas, chase problems, which are everywhere. Successful entrepreneurs solve problems. Every product or service can be thought of as a solution to a problem. We wanted to get from one place to another faster and invented the car; wanted to travel from one country to another faster and we created planes. Working couple has a problem finding time to cook: An innovative solution was found by a Startup in Finland (See Case Study on Nordic region's entrepreneurial renaissance in Section 6.4).

9. IMPROVE AN EXISTING SOLUTION

Many successful Startups were not the first in their market segment. Before Google, there were popular search engines like AltaVista and Yahoo. But they got lost in integrating news, weather, sports etc. on their homepage. Google simplified the search function.

10. ADAPTING EXISTING SOLUTIONS FROM OTHER COUNTRIES

Some ventures attempt localization of successful ventures abroad. SnapDeal is a Groupon clone in India with localized content and features. Google's clone Baidu has been a great success in China.

17
Idea Screening

An important principle of idea screening is that there are no right or wrong answers in an idea evaluation exercise, only an informed judgment that an idea will succeed or fail.

1. Does the new idea represent a good fit with the capabilities of the founder/founding team? Such capabilities include the ability to mobilize the required funds, professional competencies (including that of the professional team to be assembled to execute the plan), interests and personal qualities.
2. Is the idea feasible in the market place?
3. Is it technically feasible? Whether the solution for the customer's problem can actually be created within the parameters set – capital investment, process technology, equipment, cost of production, product quality, price, skill-sets required etc.
4. Is the opportunity worth investing in? Investment covers capital - promoters', outside investors', institutions' - the time, energy, effort and reputation of a set of people.
5. Is the potential profit level commensurate with the associated business risks? How does it compare with that of competing investment opportunities?
6. Will the opportunity for profits be sustainable over a reasonable length of time? The opportunity can be short-lived, if more powerful competition moves in.
7. Is it amenable to financing?

18
Ten Steps To Launching A Business

(In reality, it could well be 10 × 10 steps!)

1. Write a Business Plan (BP), the written guide to help you map out how you will start and run your enterprise.
2. Check with the relevant Government departments and industry associations to get free training and counseling services to fine-tune the BP.
3. Talk to a mentor who is familiar with the process of setting up a business and the industry your enterprise belongs to.
4. Finalize the financing plan and funding arrangements.
5. Determine the legal structure of your business - Sole Proprietorship, Limited Liability Partnership or Private Limited Company.
6. Register a business name.
7. Register for Central/State taxes.
8. Obtain business license/permit.
9. Learn employer responsibilities.
10. Initiate such steps as envisaged in the BP: Recruit the initial staff; acquire the site/industrial plot/shed; begin the construction of factory; tie-up the utilities; order plant and machinery; take out insurance plans for the physical assets being created/acquired; commission the project with the full complement of manpower; translate the marketing plan into action.

For a detailed checklist of step-by-step process for starting a new business in India visit www.smallb.sidbi.in.

PART V
Business Plan: Purpose, Structure and Content

"People don't plan to fail, they fail to plan" —Winston Churchill

"By failing to prepare, you are preparing to fail" —Benjamin Franklin

19
Business Plans

19.1 INTRODUCTION TO BUSINESS PLANS

Every business has some degree of risks to it; in fact, the range of risks an existing or a new enterprise could encounter is indeed wide. There is no way you can eliminate all the risks. The trick is not avoiding risks but anticipating, understanding and managing risks. Good planning improves the chance of your success. In fact, the high mortality rate of Startups is largely due to inadequate planning.

You need a map to help you find the route to an unknown destination. You need a Business Plan (BP) to help you determine in which direction to go to get your business up and running.

Preparing a BP is a vital step in the process of planning a new business. A BP captures every relevant aspect of a new investment plan including market potential, choice of technology, location, scale of operation, plant and machinery, input requirements, manpower, capital costs, operating costs and profitability.

The real value of creating a BP is not in having a document in hand; the value lies in the process of researching and thinking about your business in a structured/systematic manner leading to an objective assessment of the planned project in its entirety. This format of the BP is set essentially from the perspective of a new enterprise, as opposed to expansion/diversification of an existing entity.

> **Getting to the bottom of a given problem: "Five Whys"**
>
> (Entrepreneur.com – Sid Kemp, Mar 26, 2009)
>
> Asking, "Why is this happening" 5 times.
>
> Example: "Projects often run late"
>
> 1. Why did the project run late?
>
> *We didn't know all that we had to do. We missed the deadline.*
>
> 2. Why didn't you know what you needed to do?
>
> *We didn't sit down and write up a plan.*
>
> 3. Why didn't you write up a plan?
>
> *We didn't think it was worth the time.*
>
> 4. Why didn't you think it was worth the time?
>
> *We were running late after delays in other projects, we started late.*
>
> 5. Why were you running late on other projects?
>
> *Because we didn't sit down and write up a plan and missed our deadline.*

19.2 WHAT IS A BUSINESS PLAN?

Business Plan is different from a Feasibility Report (FR) or Detailed Project Report (DPR). A FR/DPR has an investigating function. The feasibility study analyzes several alternatives or methods of achieving business success and identifies the best possible model. It seeks to answer the central question: Is the proposed venture viable commercially, technically and financially? To save time and cost, as a practice, a pre-feasibility study is conducted to assess the relative merits of a set of business ideas or scenarios before a full-blown feasibility study.

A BP is prepared only after the business is deemed to be feasible in all respects with the aid of a Feasibility Report. However, for the sake of clarity and comprehensiveness the version of BP presented below incorporates the core elements of a Feasibility Report.

A BP is a blue print for action, a roadmap that describes where you are going and how you are going to get there. It defines your business, identifies your goals. It embodies the techno-commercial viability analysis of an investment plan.

A BP can be conceived to be a collection of sub-plans: Strategic plan/ investment plan/marketing plan/ financial plan/ production plan/human resources plan/growth plan.

Strategy represents a set of general rules for realizing the goals. Effective implementation of the strategy translates the general rules into specific decisions and actions. The strategic direction of the project must make sense within the company's market and industry environment.

BP as an analytical tool has two basic purposes: **Communication and Management & Planning**.

It is a presentation device meeting the needs of specific target audiences and purposes:

a) Investors looking for the quality of management, uniqueness of the product and technology, feasibility of achieving the forecasts, profitability and, most of all, the details of the projected returns on their investment and timeframes for getting the money back.

b) Bankers focusing on when and how the principal and interest will be repaid and availability of collateral to cover any loan losses.

c) Strategic alliances for joint research, product development and marketing.

d) Mergers and alliances: Acquisition as a means of expansion; divestiture to have liquidity. In both cases, BP to be used as a screening tool.

e) Customer and distributor relationships

f) Management team when being hired.

As a Management and Planning Tool, it helps:

1. Set short-term and long-term goals in terms of product range, production capacity, geographical coverage, resources to be acquired, revenue stream, profitability etc.

2. Establish timelines and milestones.

3. Anticipate, monitor and evaluate your progress.

4. Commit the entire management team to the same goals.

5. Hold the employees accountable for results.
6. Guide you through the various phases of your business.
7. Identify roadblocks and fashion responses; make mid-course corrections, if required.

19.3 WHAT IS A GOOD BUSINESS PLAN?

Simple, Specific, Realistic and Complete

1. Business writing to be clear, concise and easy to understand and act upon
2. Concrete and measurable objectives: Specific activities, specific dates of completion, specific persons responsible for each activity and specific budgets.
3. Sales goals, expense budgets, milestone dates etc. to be realistic; unrealistic goals kill plans and projects even before they take off.
4. Takes into account all relevant elements of the proposed activity.

Reality check – Are you fooling yourself? Expect the unexpected: A good Business Plan anticipates possible challenges and includes a variety of action plans for meeting those challenges.

A good BP should leave the following conclusions with the prospective investors:

1. Basic business concept makes sense; the product proposition offers real competitive advantage; market prospects are good.
2. Business has been thoroughly thought through
3. Management is capable
4. Financial projections are realistic
5. Investors have a good chance of getting decent returns
6. A realistic picture of the risks inherent in the business

Investors do not invest in BP; they invest in people, the idea, the technology and the track record of the promoters. A BP shall define and explain the different components.

19.4 OUTLINE OF A BUSINESS PLAN

I. COVER SHEET

a) Name of the company, address, telephones, e-mail

b) A statement instructing readers to keep the contents confidential.

II. EXECUTIVE SUMMARY

This section is more important than any other. All those who examine a BP read this. Hence, it must be crisp, complete and realistic, as the rest of the report. If it is not, not many will continue reading. About five pages should be fine.

Executive Summary is a concise form of the BP covering such key points as:

Brief history of the enterprise; and the legal structure (Proprietorship/Partnership/Private Ltd. or Public Ltd)

1. Background of the promoters and the top talents to be acquired
2. Business concept
3. Market prospects
4. Technical feasibility
5. Financial viability
6. Exit Strategy: Options for the investors to take the money out
7. Scheduling of activities: Important milestones
8. Contingencies: What-if-planning

III. TYPE OF BUSINESS

Manufacturing product/Delivering services/Brokering information/Distributing or retailing goods

IV. MARKET FEASIBILITY

Refer *How Winners Win Customer Loyalty in* Chapter 7 under Part II.

V. TECHNICAL FEASIBILITY (Relates mainly to Manufacturing)

The key issues underlying the assessment of technical feasibility of a new venture are:

a) Choice of technology

b) Scale of operation

c) Plant & machinery

d) Choice of location

e) Management team

f) Manpower

g) Plant layout

h) Procedures for production, purchase and inventory management and quality control

i) Optimizing the use of utilities and other inputs

j) Scheduling and monitoring

Brief discussions on the important parameters follow.

CHOICE OF TECHNOLOGY

Process technology profoundly affects many vital aspects of a manufacturing enterprise:

a) Operational efficiency (the input-output system), which will determine the competitive power of the enterprise, the market share and the level of profitability.

b) Investment cost of the project via the cost of plant & machinery compatible to the technology as well as the cost of technology.

c) Product quality, functionality and features

d) Life of a project: Enterprises based on outmoded technologies will give way to those incorporating advanced technologies because better technology yields larger output for the same level of input or the same level of output for lesser input/lower quality input or uses up less of labour, power and fuel. Of course, better technology does also improve product quality.

e) The product (as against the process) can also incorporate appropriate technology; many 'smart' white goods like washing machines or refrigerators have embedded technologies

f) Scale of operation

Sources: Individual experts/consulting groups/existing manufacturers/machinery suppliers/research labs/R&D initiative.

Pitfalls to be guarded against: Unproven/proven only at lab or pilot plant scale; without performance guarantee; not compatible with local materials; high cost; threat of obsolescence.

SCALE OF OPERATION

The production capacity of a project is determined by the chosen process technology (many technologies specify a minimum capacity below which it is inefficient or infeasible), the size of the potential market for the new enterprise in the immediate future and the investment capability of the promoter.

Scale of operation has a bearing on the cost of production. Higher the capacity, lower the unit cost. Cost of production impacts price which, in turn, may determine market share and profitability.

If the capacity is larger than your market, there will be under-utilization of installed capacity. It means the project has to carry the cost of the capacity that is not being used. If the market grows faster than what you had assumed, you can quickly expand your capacity; you can also explore tapping other sources of supply to meet your customer requirements till your additional capacity comes on stream.

MACHINERY & EQUIPMENT

Machinery & Equipment is the single largest component in the project cost, especially for a manufacturing firm. Precautions to be taken include:

1. Compatible with the chosen process/capacity of the plant
2. Reputation of the supplier: There can be a trade-off between cost and reliability; even if more expensive sourcing from reputed suppliers is a smart idea.
3. Performance guarantee, delivery schedule, spare parts supply

4. Negotiated price
5. Internal balance among equipment configuration
6. If second-hand, careful study of residual life with the help of Chartered Engineers

CHOICE OF LOCATION

Location requirements vary from industry to industry. Some are location-neutral and others are location-bound. When the process is 'weight-losing' (i.e., the weight of the end product is only a fraction of the collective weight of the major inputs as in steel-making), the project should be closer to source of such inputs. When the process is 'weight-gaining' (i.e., when the end-product is the outcome of integrating sub-assemblies and components), the project should be closer to the market. IT industry tends to gravitate towards cities with adequate supply of professionals, good technical as well as general infrastructure including good housing, educational facilities and urban amenities.

Regions are differently endowed with respect to the needs of the industry. Location does affect the capital as well as operating cost of a project.

Careful location study to optimize the cost of transportation of inputs and end products and to meet the special requirements of a given project is, therefore, very essential. It would be helpful if the chosen location is one where the kind of people you want to hire are comfortable living.

The location study takes into account such factors as:

1. Access to market, raw materials, transportation and qualified labour pool
2. Regulatory requirements
3. Governmental incentives
4. Community receptiveness to having the business being located in the identified site

MANAGEMENT TEAM

1. Identify the key skills your type of business must have and acquire what you or other members of the founding team lack: Experiences

in solving customer problems (marketing skills), process technology, manufacturing operation and financial management.

2. Define the roles and responsibilities of all key functionaries.
3. A healthy HR policy: Compensation package to be performance-driven and competitive enough to attract and retain the right talents.

OPERATIONS

Refer *How Best to Manage Operations* in Chapter 10 under Part II.

SCHEDULING AND MONITORING

Improper scheduling and inadequate control and monitoring cause time/cost over-run. PERT/CPM techniques provide means to control/monitor projects.

VI. FINANCIAL VIABILITY

Refer *How Best to Manage Money* in Chapter 9 under Part II.

VII. VISION AND MISSION STATEMENTS

Management Gurus and Consultants often exhort the need for well-articulated Vision & Mission Statements. Business Plan, in fact, begins with these statements. It may, however, be conceded that the vision and mission statements are not all that easy to define or differentiate.

1. VISION STATEMENT:

In one succinct sentence or two, describe the central purpose of your business; a declaration of what the business aspires to be; a coherent set of values for your company. It gives shape and direction to the organization's future. Your vision statement is your inspiration, the framework for all your strategic planning. It answers the question, where do we want to go? "A vision is your mental picture of future success".

The employees must feel proud and excited. A vision statement is for you and the other members of your company, not necessarily for your customers.

To be the company that best understands and satisfies the product, service and self-fulfillment needs of women globally

—Avon

People working together as one global enterprise for aerospace leadership

—Boeing

Be the global leader in customer value

—Caterpillar

The vision of DuPont is to be the world's most dynamic science company creating sustainable solutions essential to a better, safer and healthier life for people everywhere

—Du Pont

2. MISSION STATEMENT:

Mission Statement is a precise description of the business: What it is, what it does, what it is aiming to deliver, to whom, why it makes a difference and what it aspires to accomplish. It is a definition of "why" the organization exists.

Every enterprise has a mission and a story to tell, even a Startup - its past, its future. Every company has to have a distinctive value proposition that clearly meets consumer needs better than the competition.

Describe what your enterprise/business will look like in, say, 5 years time, the likely size and the nature, breadth and depth of operations.

Our mission is simply to offer our customers the most binocular aperture, at the highest quality for the lowest price

—Big Binoculars

We will market the most appealing and widely worn casual clothing in the world. We will clothe the world

—Levi Strauss

Our mission is to inform, inspire and empower people and organizations to be their best - both personally and professionally

—Success Network

Our mission is to be consumer's first choice for food, delivering products of outstanding quality and great service at a competitive cost through working faster, simpler and together

—J. Sainsbury

To develop, sell and install easy-to-use, customized, full-featured accounting software for small and medium sized businesses whose current off-the-shelf systems do not meet their needs

—An Accounting software developer

To provide strategic planning services that improves the performance and efficiency of small business start-ups and increases their chances of finding suitable financing

—Business Consultant

To create, manufacture and market high quality educational toys and games that children will find enjoyable and challenging and will be a good value for the purchaser

—An educational-toy maker

We are a market - focused, process - centered organization that develops and delivers innovative solutions to our customers, consistently out performs our peers, produces predictable earnings for our shareholders and provides a dynamic and challenging environment for our employees

—Ashland, a global petroleum company

To be the most effective law firm on the most difficult cases involving US law

—Cravath, Swaine and Moore (Law Firm)

PART VI

Is Entrepreneurship for You? Do You Have What It Takes?

20
Testing for Entrepreneurial Prowess

20.1 ENTREPRENEURIAL TESTING IS NOT AN EXACT SCIENCE

Studies of **successful entrepreneurs** reveal common characteristics – family background, experiences, motivations, personality traits, behaviours, values and beliefs.

It would be instructive to ask yourself a set of questions before you choose an entrepreneurial career. Not that answers to such questions will open up an entrepreneurial path. There is no way of knowing whether anyone has the potential to be a successful entrepreneur. No test can predict your success. At best, it can only give you an idea whether you will have a head start or a handicap with which to work.

Questions and the select self-rating tests that follow could help assess your resolve. Provided, of course, you are absolutely honest with yourself when you answer them!

20.2 THIRTEEN QUESTIONS TO TEST YOUR RESOLVE AND RESOURCES

1. Are you ready for a lifetime of commitment?
2. Do you have the physical and emotional stamina to ignore security and an attractive career for a highly demanding, uncertain world of entrepreneurship?
3. Are you familiar with the type of activity you plan to start?
4. Does the chosen idea suit your personality and interests and do you truly believe in what you plan to do?

5. Do you have the typical traits of successful entrepreneurs: Desire, drive, discipline, determination, curiosity, insight/intuition, self-confidence, optimism, people skills, resilience?
6. Are you realistic about your strengths in terms of your confidence in mobilizing the required finance as well as attracting, retaining and empowering the right professional team?
7. Can you afford to lose the money you need to invest in the business?
8. Can you maintain tight control over the money?
9. Do people you care about – your family and friends – support your decision to pursue an entrepreneurial career as well as your chosen business?
10. Do you have the support of a Mentor, a business veteran who provides objective, unvarnished, unbiased, direct/blunt advice and direction?
11. Do you seek advice and feedback?
12. Do you listen to your critics and do you apply what you learn?
13. Is the ecosystem you plan to operate in is essentially pro-enterprise?

If your answers to the above questions are YES, you have a more than even chance of becoming a successful entrepreneur.

Provided, of course, that you can pick, most of the time, if not all the time, the best from among the different options that present themselves every step of the way!

Such options relate to a wide range of vital aspects of a given project: Choice of product and its features or technology or scale of operation or location or financing pattern. In fact, the concept of what is the 'best' has to be contextualized; what is best today need not necessarily be so a year down the road.

If hundreds of thousands of entrepreneurs have done it before under conditions ranging from excellent to lukewarm to indifferent to hostile, there is no reason why you can't!

Some more questions to ponder over before you start

1. Why do I want to start a business?
    a) To make a living
    b) To get rich

c) To pursue a dream
   d) To exploit an opportunity
   e) To improve the world
   f) Fast track career path
   g) No viable alternative
2. a) What price am I willing to pay?
   a) Long working hours
   b) Less time with family
   c) Financial uncertainty
3. How much risk can I take?
4. How will I finance my business?
5. Can I do it alone? (Sharing the burden can enhance the chances of success)
6. What are my GO/NO GO criteria? Deadline?
   a) For an acceptable business plan
   b) For getting funding
   c) For a technical proof-of-concept for the product
7. How will I market my product?

20.3 SMALL BUSINESS READINESS ASSESSMENT TOOL

Here are four tests designed to test your readiness to take on entrepreneurship as a career options. These are only indicative. As stated earlier, no test can predict your success.

I. ONLINE TEST DESIGNED BY SMALL BUSINESS ADMINISTRATION, USA

To get an assessment of your level of readiness take the test at http://www.sba.gov/assessmenttool/index.html.

II. GAUGING ENTREPRENEURIAL PERSONALITY

This is a questionnaire designed by Thomas Duening, Ira A. Fulton School of Engineering of the Arizona State University, based on the research conducted by Prof. W. Kummerle, Harvard Business School:

1. Are you comfortable stretching rules?

   Rules are stretched or interpreted creatively; successful entrepreneurs resort to some audacious tactic to get their idea launched.

2. Are you prepared to make enemies?

   Successful entrepreneurs are not afraid to make enemies in the pursuit of their goals. They have no great needs for approval.

3. Do you have the patience to start small?

   "Get big fast" philosophy can result in burning up the capital without reaching the goal. Patience is a virtue for Startups.

4. Are you willing to shift strategies quickly?

   In the world of business things keep changing and, therefore, no strategy is forever. Keep changing to meet the market requirements.

5. Are you a closer?

   Successful entrepreneurs know how to close deals. In Startup ventures, it means being comfortable repeatedly making life-or-death decisions without sufficient information.

IF YOU ANSWERED "NO" TO ANY OF THE QUESTIONS, YOU MAY WANT TO THINK HARD ABOUT WHETHER ENTREPRENEURSHIP IS RIGHT FOR YOU.

III. SELF-RATING OF TYPICAL TRAITS OF SUCCESSFUL ENTREPRENEURS

An enlarged version of the self-rating format designed by Fred Diulus, CEO, Global Academy Online ZeroMillions.com (See the 11 traits in all Caps)

Rate each of the following traits (circle one choice of the score) as you believe it relates to you using the following scale: +2 = I am very strong in this characteristic; +1= I possess this characteristic; 0 = I don't know; -1= I have very little of this characteristic; -2 = I do not possess this characteristic

SCORING

Your score will fall between -60 to + 60. A high positive score demonstrates you have the characteristics needed to succeed as an entrepreneur.

TRAITS	SCORE				
CREATIVE/INNOVATIVE	+2	+1	0	-1	-2
RISK-TAKING	+2	+1	0	-1	-2
SELF-CONFIDENT	+2	+1	0	-1	-2
DYNAMIC	+2	+1	0	-1	-2
LIKES TO LEAD OTHERS	+2	+1	0	-1	-2
MARKET SAVVY	+2	+1	0	-1	-2
RESOURCEFUL	+2	+1	0	-1	-2
PERSEVERE	+2	+1	0	-1	-2
OPTIMISTIC	+2	+1	0	-1	-2
KNOWLEDGEABLE	+2	+1	0	-1	-2
HIGH ENERGY LEVEL	+2	+1	0	-1	-2
Tenacious	+2	+1	0	-1	-2
Hardworking	+2	+1	0	-1	-2
Disciplined	+2	+1	0	-1	-2
Time-conscious	+2	+1	0	-1	-2
Adaptable/Flexible	+2	+1	0	-1	-2
Competitive	+2	+1	0	-1	-2
Self-starter/Initiative	+2	+1	0	-1	-2
Enthusiastic	+2	+1	0	-1	-2
Pragmatic/Realistic	+2	+1	0	-1	-2
Result/Action-oriented	+2	+1	0	-1	-2
Willingness to learn	+2	+1	0	-1	-2
Sense of urgency	+2	+1	0	-1	-2
Strong need to achieve	+2	+1	0	-1	-2
Emotional stability	+2	+1	0	-1	-2

Being independent	+2	+1	0	-1	-2
Attention to detail	+2	+1	0	-1	-2
Highly motivated/ambitious	+2	+1	0	-1	-2
Networking skills	+2	+1	0	-1	-2
Attracting and retaining the right team	+2	+1	0	-1	-2

IV. WHAT IS YOUR E.Q. (ENTREPRENEURIAL QUOTIENT)?

Northwestern Mutual Life, USA, devised this test. The test is to help you see how you compare with others who have been successful entrepreneurs.

Add or subtract your score cumulatively as you evaluate yourself:

1. Significantly high numbers of entrepreneurs are children of first-generation Americans. If your parents immigrated to the United States, score 1. If not, score -1. (Relevant only to US citizens)

2. Successful entrepreneurs are not, as a rule, top achievers in school. If you were a top student, subtract 4. If not, add 4.

3. Entrepreneurs are not especially enthusiastic about participating in group activities in school. If you enjoyed group activities - clubs, team sports, double dates - subtract 1. If not, add 1.

4. Studies of entrepreneurs show that, as youngsters, they often preferred to be alone. Did you prefer to be alone when young? If so, add 1. If not, subtract 1

5. Those who started enterprises during childhood - lemonade stands, family newspapers, and greeting card sales - or ran for elected office at school can add 2, because enterprise usually can be traced to an early age. If you didn't initiate enterprises, subtract 2.

6. Stubbornness as a child seems to translate into determination to do things one's own way - a hallmark of proven entrepreneurs. If you were stubborn as a child, add 1. If not, subtract 1.

7. Caution may involve an unwillingness to take risks, a handicap for those embarking on previously uncharted territory. Were you a cautious youngster? If yes, deduct 4. If no, add 4.

8. If you were daring or adventuresome, add 4 more.
9. Entrepreneurs often have the faith to pursue different paths despite the opinions of others. If the opinions of others matter a lot to you, subtract 1. If not, add 1.
10. Being tired of a daily routine often precipitates an entrepreneur's decision to start an enterprise. If changing your daily routine would be an important motivation for starting your own enterprise, add 2. If not, subtract 2.
11. Yes, you really enjoy work. But are you willing to work overnight? If yes, add 2. If no, subtract 2.
12. If you are willing to work as long as it takes with little or no sleep to finish a job, add four 4.
13. Entrepreneurs generally enjoy their type of work so much they move from one project to another - non-stop. When you complete a project successfully, do you immediately start another? If yes, add 2. If no, subtract 2.
14. Successful entrepreneurs are willing to use their savings to finance a project. If you are willing to commit your savings to start a business, add 2. If not, subtract 2.
15. Would you be willing to borrow from others? Then add 2 more. If not, subtract 2.
16. If your business should fail, would you immediately start working on another? If yes, add 4. If no, subtract 4.
17. Or, if you would immediately start looking for a job with a regular paycheck, subtract 1 more.
18. Do you believe being an entrepreneur is risky? If yes, subtract 2. If no, add 2.
19. Many entrepreneurs put their long-term and short-term goals in writing. If you do, add 1. If you don't, subtract 1.
20. Handling cash flow can be critical to entrepreneurial success. Do you believe you have the ability to deal with cash flow in a professional manner? If so, add 2. If not, subtract 2.
21. Entrepreneurial personalities seem to be easily bored. If you are easily bored, add 2. If not, subtract

22. Optimism can fuel the drive to press for success in uncharted waters. If you're an optimist, add 2. Pessimist, subtract 2.

Your Entrepreneurial Quotient (EQ)

a) If you scored +35 or more, you have everything going for you. You ought to achieve spectacular entrepreneurial success (barring acts of God or other variables beyond your control)

b) If you scored +15 to +34, your background, skills and talents give you excellent chances for success in your own business. You should go far.

c) If you scored 0 to +15, you have a head start of ability and/or experience in running a business and ought to be successful in opening an enterprise of your own if you apply yourself and learn the necessary skills to make it happen

d) If you scores 0 to -15, you might be able to make a go of it if you ventured on your own, but you would have to work extra hard to compensate for a lack of built-in advantages and skills that give others a leg up in beginning their own business

e) If you scored -15 to -43, your talents probably lie elsewhere. You ought to consider whether building your own business is what you really want to do, because you may find yourself swimming against the tide if you make the attempt. Another work arrangement - working for a company or for someone else, or developing a career in a profession or an area of technical expertise - may be far more congenial to you and allow you to enjoy a lifestyle appropriate to your abilities and interests.

www.ingramcontent.com/pod-product-compliance
Lightning Source LLC
Chambersburg PA
CBHW020636220526
45464CB00001B/170